WEIGHT WATCHERS
Slim Ways With Pasta

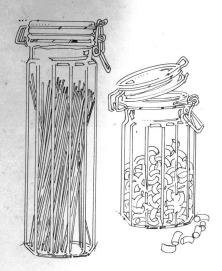

AN NAL BOOK

NAL BOOKS
Published by the Penguin Group
Penguin Books USA Inc., 375 Hudson Street
New York, New York 10014, U.S.A.
Penguin Books Ltd, 27 Wrights Lane,
London W8 5TZ, England
Penguin Books Australia Ltd, Ringwood,
Victoria, Australia
Penguin Books Canada Ltd, 10 Alcorn Avenue,
Toronto, Ontario, Canada M4V 3B2
Penguin Books (N.Z.) Ltd, 182-190 Wairau Road,
Auckland 10, New Zealand

Penguin Books Ltd, Registered Offices:
Harmondsworth, Middlesex, England

First published by Dutton, an imprint of New American Library, a division of Penguin
Books USA Inc.

First Printing, September, 1992
10 9 8 7 6

 REGISTERED TRADEMARK—MARCA REGISTRADA

LC NUMBER 92–053538
Printed in the United States of America

Weight Watchers

Since 1963, Weight Watchers has grown from a handful of people to a million enrollments. Today, Weight Watchers is one of the recognized leaders in the weight-control field. Members are a diverse group from youths, 10 and over, to senior citizens attending meetings virtually around the globe. Growing numbers of people purchase and enjoy our popular expanding line of convenience foods, best-selling cookbooks, personal calendar planners and both audio and video exercise tapes.

To learn about the extensive variety of foods and menus available to Weight Watchers members, we invite you to join the Weight Watchers meeting nearest you. There, under the guidance and support of a trained leader, you'll learn how to lose weight and how to keep it off.

This book was created con amore *by a group of dedicated, health-conscious pasta-lovers: chefs Linda Rosensweig, Joel Jason, Joyce Kenneally and Phyllis Kohn; editors Lee Haiken, Mary Novitsky, Stephanie Graziadio, Liz George, Susan Rees and Lee Randall; pasta-maker A.J. Battifarano; art directors Neil Stuart and Shelley Stansfield; designers Lisa Realmuto and Jennifer Simpson; and illustrator Alice Simpson.*

Contents

Introduction

In Italy, where there are almost 2,000 different names for pasta shapes, people are so passionate about pasta that it even has a patron saint, Saint Stephano, and a mascot, the whimsical Punchinella! Contrary to the popular belief that Marco Polo introduced pasta to Italy when he brought it back from China, some historians have suggested that predating Marco Polo by about 1,600 years is an ancient relief, probably Etruscan, clearly depicting pasta-making tools. Whatever its origin, it wasn't until the Industrial Revolution that commercially made pasta became available to the masses. An entire street culture grew up around making, cooking and eating pasta, and it became the street food of the Neapolitans. In America, Thomas Jefferson heralded the arrival of pasta when he imported a spaghetti machine from Naples and, in 1802, served a macaroni and cheese casserole to dinner guests.

Why is this simple combination of flour and eggs one of the world's most popular foods? Inexpensive, easy to prepare, an ideal foil for seasonings and flavorings, endlessly versatile as a main or side dish, in salads, soups or even desserts, pasta has become an important pantry staple. Indeed, with a package of pasta in your kitchen, you always have a ready meal. There is more to pasta, however, than just being delicious and beloved. Nutritionists today agree that healthy meal planning should emphasize fruits, vegetables and grain products, choosing from a wide variety to help supply the more than 40 nutrients your body requires. Carbohydrates, like pasta, provide a major source of energy and are also good sources of vitamins, minerals and fiber. It is recommended that 50-60 percent of your daily calories come from carbohydrate foods: fruits, vegetables and grain products. On the Weight Watchers Food Plan, pasta is found on the Bread List, and 3/4 ounce uncooked pasta or 1/2 cup cooked (except for tiny shapes, like pastina and orzo) provides one Bread Selection™.

All recipes in this book conform to the Weight Watchers Personal Choice® Full Choice Option, Level 2, Week 3. We hope that you have many delicious and healthy meals with them.

About our Recipes

To help you fit these recipes into the Food Plan, Selection™ Information is provided for each recipe, followed by a per-serving nutritional analysis of calories, protein, fat, carbohydrate, calcium, sodium, cholesterol and dietary fiber for the recipe exactly as written. Bear in mind that adding anything, such as extra salt or fat, will alter that analysis. To create recipes with a healthy nutrition profile, we've used a variety of ingredients like egg substitutes, reduced-fat cheeses and low-sodium broths. Any recipe which reflects a reduction of sodium or cholesterol or derives 30 percent or less of calories from fat will be so noted at the end.

Reduced fat indicates that 30 percent or less of the calories come from fat.

Reduced sodium means that a recipe providing 2 or more Proteins contains 400 milligrams or less of sodium per serving. All other recipes so noted contain 200 milligrams or less of sodium per serving.

Reduced cholesterol means that a recipe providing 2 or more Proteins contains 50 milligrams or less of cholesterol per serving. All other recipes so noted contain 25 milligrams or less of cholesterol per serving.

Kitchen Notes

Whether you're a novice cook or a kitchen pro, it's always a good idea to read a recipe through before getting started.

* Check to make sure you have all the ingredients, assemble everything within easy reach, and allow enough time for preparation and cooking so that the dish is ready when you want to serve it.

* Thawing frozen items in the refrigerator or microwave oven is safer than leaving them out on a counter.

* Measure or weigh ingredients carefully for best results and accuracy of Selection Information and nutrition analysis. Where amounts are called for in ounces or pounds, weigh these ingredients on a food scale. Measure liquids in a standard glass or clear plastic measuring cup. Use standard measuring spoons for amounts less than 1/4 cup.

* Measure dry ingredients in metal or plastic cups, available in $1/4$, $1/3$, $1/2$, $2/3$, $3/4$ and 1-cup sizes. Fill cups or measuring spoons and level tops with a knife or spatula.

* A dash of something is about 1/16 of a teaspoon (one-half of a 1/8 teaspoon or one-fourth of a 1/4 teaspoon). A pinch is the amount you can hold between two fingers.

* When preparing a recipe for more than one serving, mix the ingredients well. When serving, divide evenly so that each serving has an equal amount of all ingredients.

* If you are going to chill or freeze a prepared recipe, allow the food to cool slightly. You can hasten cooling of large quantities by dividing the food into smaller containers. By refrigerating or freezing serving-size amounts in microwave-safe containers, you'll always have a food-plan right meal for those no-time-to-cook days.

Ingredient Notes

Cheese: Many of our recipes call for reduced-fat cheese, which is often lower in sodium as well.

Citrus zest: The bright-colored outer skin of citrus fruits without the pith (white membrane).

Egg substitutes: Look for these in the freezer case of your supermarket, and keep a carton on hand in your own freezer. They are made mostly of egg white and are cholesterol-free. Thaw before using.

Fruits: Fruits and fruit juices (canned or frozen) should not contain added sugar. Look for fruits packed in juice, a juice blend or water.

Ground meat: Look for the leanest ground beef, veal, lamb and pork in the meat case if you want to keep your fat and cholesterol intake down. There is plenty of flavor in other ingredients, so you'll never miss the fat.

Oils: Vegetable oils (safflower, sunflower, soybean, corn, canola) have specific properties that make them work well in certain recipes and are often interchangeable. Olive, walnut and peanut oils have very distinctive flavors, so use these when specified. In recipes calling for sesame oil, choose the dark variety, which is made from toasted sesame seeds, has a rich amber color and characteristic sesame flavor and aroma. Refrigerate nut and seed oils after opening to prevent spoilage.

Peppers: Chili peppers contain volatile oils that can make your skin and eyes burn. It's a good idea to wear rubber gloves when handling them, and be careful not to touch your eyes or face. When you're finished, thoroughly wash your hands, the knife and cutting board to remove all traces of the peppers.

Seasonings: Many of our recipes call for fresh herbs, which will add a special flavor to the dish. You might want to experiment with tastes to get just the one you and your family like. If fresh herbs are not available, substitute one-third the amount dried (1 tablespoon fresh to 1 teaspoon dried).

Shellfish: Always buy live clams and mussels with tightly closed shells. If you spot a slightly open shell, tap it hard. If it doesn't snap shut, discard it.

11 The Many Shapes of Pasta

Although it seems hard to imagine, there are approximately 600 different pasta shapes worldwide, some 150 of which are available in the United States. Most consumers, though, will only have 30-40 varieties to choose from at their grocery stores...but that certainly seems to be more than enough!

Because of similar characteristics, certain pastas can be substituted for others in recipes. So if you can't find the pasta you need for your favorite recipe, don't be afraid to be creative; sometimes its fun to switch shapes just to make the meal more interesting.

Although there are no hard and fast rules for selecting the perfect pasta shape for your meal, each type of pasta, due to its size, thickness and shape, lends itself differently to various sauces. To help make choosing or substituting pastas a little less confusing, we've included a glossary of the more common varieties and what basic sauces they're best suited for. We've also, where appropriate, included the origin of the pasta name—it is often very illustrative.

SPAGHETTI: The word spaghetti, *in Italiano*, means "a length of cord." And since all of the spaghetti family are long, cylindrical lengths of pasta, the name seems to fit. These pastas lend themselves very well to lightly sauced dishes. Thick meat sauces are not recommended for this type of pasta: Since the pasta is so thin, the sauce is not evenly distributed and the meat tends to sink to the bottom of the bowl. Spaghetti works well with oil-based, butter or tomato sauces, which will cover the pasta without oversaucing. Some of the more common spaghetti shapes are, from thinnest to thickest:

Capelli d'Angelo or

    Capellini ("fine hairs"): also known as Angel Hair

      Spaghettini ("little lengths of cord")

        Spaghetti

        Vermicelli

Fusilli Bucati: twisted, or spiral-shaped spaghetti

FETTUCCINE: To a *compatriota*, fettuccine means "small ribbons." This family of pasta is long and flat, and ranges in size from $1/16$ of an inch to 3" wide. The thinner of these pastas, such as linguine and tagliatelle, work well with clam sauces, and both fettuccine and tagliatelle (which can be substituted for each other) hold creamy sauces very well. From narrowest to widest, the more common ribbon pastas are:

Linguine ("little tongues"): long, flat, spaghetti-like pasta

    Tagliatelle

      Fettuccine: $1/8$-$1/4$" wide

        Pappardelle: $1/2$" wide, often with a crinkled edge

        Lasagna: 2-3" wide; available with a curly or plain edge

MACARONI: The tubular pastas are referred to as "maccheroni," or macaroni. They may be as long as spaghetti and fettuccine, or can be cut—"tagliare"—to 2". Ribbed or grooved versions are labeled "rigati." Their curves and crannies lend themselves to thick, chunky vegetable or meat sauces. They are also delicious in baked dishes.

Mostaccioli ("small mustaches"): smooth exterior, 2" long

Mostaccioli Rigati: cut, ridged macaroni

Penne ("quills"): smooth exterior, about 2" long

Rigatoni: large, grooved macaroni

Ziti ("bridegrooms"): either straight or slightly curved macaroni; can be very long

Ziti Rigati: cut, ridged ziti

Ziti Tagliati: ziti that has been cut into straight pieces, about 2" long

All zitis, penne and mostaccioli are interchangeable.

MISCELLANEOUS: Some fun, fanciful pastas can't be classified within the confines of geometric shapes. The smaller of these pastas, such as elbows, radiatore and conchiglie, are ideal for cheese sauces, like macaroni and cheese casseroles. The larger tubular and shell pastas are perfect for stuffing and baking; and for a different twist on pasta salad, try rotelle, farfalle or orecchiette.

Cannelloni: a large, bluntly cut, smooth tube, suitable for stuffing

Cavatelli: small, narrow, closely wrapped shells

Conchiglie ("shells"): medium-size shells

Conchiglioni: large shells, suitable for stuffing

Farfalle ("butterflies"): also known as bow ties

Fusilli/Tagliati/Rotelle/Rotini: spiral-shaped pasta, also called corkscrews

Gnocchi: shells, similar to cavatelli, but thicker and traditionally made with a potato dough

THE MANY SHAPES OF PASTA
Slim Ways with Pasta

Manicotti: large tube similar to cannelloni, but with ends cut on a diagonal; these are suitable for stuffing and may also be rigati

Orecchiette ("little ears"): disc-shaped pasta, holds thick sauces well

Radiatore ("little radiators"): grooved and loosely rolled in upon itself

Ravioli: square pasta stuffed with cheese, meat, seafood or vegetable fillings

Rotelle ("wagon wheels"): also called ruote

SMALL PASTA: These are often used in soups and broths. Delicate pastina works well in light broths and soups; larger ditalini and tubetti are perfect for thick, hearty soups, like minestrone. These versatile pastas are also a wonderful alternative to potatoes and rice as a side dish or appetizer.

Alphabets

Ancini Pepe ("peppercorns"): resemble tiny pieces of cut spaghetti

Anellini or Anelli ("little rings")

Conchiglie: small shells

Ditalini ("little thimbles"): small tubes, larger than tubetti

Orzo: rice-shaped, often called barley pasta

Pastina ("little pasta"): tiny star-shapes

Stelline ("little stars")

Tripolini ("little bows"): small, rounded bow ties

Tubetti ("little tubes")

Tubettini ("tiny tubes")

THE MANY SHAPES OF PASTA
Slim Ways with Pasta

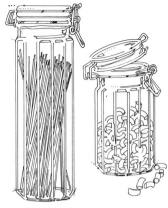

Ever since Yankee Doodle "stuck a feather in his cap and called it macaroni," Americans have been enjoying the taste of pasta. And now, with so many pasta gadgets available to the home gourmand, making fresh pasta is too easy and enjoyable to not try yourself. (See our recipes and directions, beginning on page 19.) We've included a directory of some equipment you will need if you plan to make fresh pasta and also of what you'll need to cook your pasta, dry or fresh. But if you don't have what we recommend, or can't get it, you can easily make do with what you already have. Improvisation is a part of what makes Italian cooking so good. (A little bit of this and a little bit of that add a lot of distinction to your pasta creation.) *Buona fortuna!*

Electric Pasta Machines: A good machine should feature a compartment in which the machine will mix dough ingredients and knead the dough at the flip of a switch. A few minutes later, and with another flip of a switch, your pasta machine will extrude the dough through your choice of pasta die. The best machines include a fan to dry the pasta as it is being extruded, and a good selection of pasta dies. What separates good pasta machines from truly great pasta machines, however, are two things: The fewer individual moving parts involved, the easier assembly and disassembly are, and less cleanup time needed. Also, the kneading blades within the mixing bowl should move in one direction when kneading the dough and the opposite when extruding. For instance, if the blades always move in one direction and an opening is created for the dough when it is time to extrude, there is a chance that flour will seep out during mixing time. This will alter the balance of dry and wet ingredients in the mixing bowl and make it difficult to have the right dough consistency for extrusion. All machines should include measuring cups, instructions and recipes.

Manual Pasta Machines: Although these machines take a little more work than the electric variety, they are less expensive and are worth the effort—they make beautiful pasta that you could be proud to serve to any guest. They are designed to be clamped to a table or countertop and hand-cranked to create the long sheets of dough. A dial on the side will aid in pinpointing desired dough thickness. Once the long sheets of dough are ready for shaping, they are passed through the cutting rollers that are attached to the machine. Most manual machines come with two cutting attachments or rollers (usually for spaghetti and fettuccine); other attachments for a wide variety of pasta shapes can be purchased separately. Many manufacturers also offer a motor that can be attached to the manual machine, eliminating the need to hand-crank.

Drying racks: Pasta drying racks are made of natural wood and consist of a base and individual rods that either attach to or rest upon the base. Because the rods are not permanently affixed to their base, it's easy to catch strands of pasta as they are being cut. The rods are then placed on the rack so that the pasta can hang and dry (all of which is a surprisingly quick process).

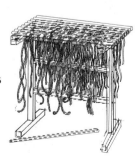

For drying short or filled pastas, you will need a clean cotton (not terry) kitchen towel or sheet and a large flat area on which to lay it out. Arrange pasta with enough space around it to allow air to circulate and dry the pasta.

Specialty Pasta Makers: There are a host of specialty machines available, such as cavatelli and gnocchi makers. Like the manual pasta maker, these attach to table or countertop and are hand-cranked. Ravioli, cavatelli and cannelloni makers are also available as small appliances. These are rectangular-shaped gadgets with the pasta forms within—almost like an ice-cube tray. Dough is placed in the tray, fillings are added, a top sheet of dough is placed and a small rolling pin (included) is rolled over the tray. Raised edges around the pasta forms aid the rolling pin in cutting and sealing the individual pastas, all in one motion.

Ravioli Cutter: If you plan to roll your own dough to make ravioli, one option for shaping and sealing is a ravioli cutter or stamp. The cutters usually have wooden handles and steel bottoms and look much like standard rubber stamps. They come in either round or square shapes and are often larger than the ravioli makers, thereby leaving a lot of room for fillings. Or, for the truly traditional, all you need is a beveled pizza cutter, which seals as it cuts.

Dough Scraper: The scrapers used for pasta largely resemble the putty knives painters use to clean walls. They have a short wooden handle and a wide steel blade. Scrapers help with moving and cutting the dough and with cleanup.

Rolling Pins: A standard rolling pin is good for rolling out pasta, but since pasta dough should ideally be rolled into very thin sheets, a pasta rolling pin, or *matarello,* is perfect. This Italian rolling pin, measuring 24 inches, is longer than the standard rolling pin; therefore, it rolls the sheet of pasta (called *sfoglia*) wider and thinner than other pins. That means less time spent rolling and re-rolling dough.

Measures: Liquid as well as dry measuring cups and spoons will be necessary to ensure proper dough consistency when following a recipe.

Mixing Bowls: Any type of bowl will do, but it is wise to have a variety of sizes and shapes. A wide shallow bowl is good for mixing ingredients for dough, a deep one for mixing fillings for stuffed pastas.

Here are a few kitchen tools that will make cooking simpler:

Large Saucepan or Stock Pot: Since this pot will be used for boiling water and cooking pasta, it should be heavy-bottomed, have at least a 4-quart capacity and a lid. Some pots come with colanders that fit right inside; pasta is cooked within the colander. These make the transition from pot to serving platter quick and easy.

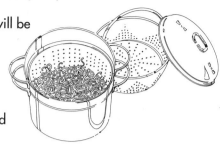

Small Saucepan or Skillet: You'll want to have your sauce simmering while you cook your pasta, so it's always good to have extra pans for that purpose.

Wooden Spoons and Forks: Wooden spoons are good for stirring short pastas and pastas for soups. Wooden forks are good for stirring the ribbon-like pastas, such as spaghetti, fettuccine and tagliatelle.

Spaghetti Rake: This combination wooden fork and spoon has 1" wooden prongs projecting from its paddle-shaped back. It is used both to stir the ribbon-like pastas, and to transfer cooked pasta to the colander for faster draining, since not all the water from the pot goes into the colander with the pasta.

Spaghetti Server: This metal or heatproof plastic variation of the spaghetti rake is shaped like a spoon, with the prongs along the perimeter. Don't let the name fool you—this server also holds short tubular and small pastas. It's perfect for taste-testing!

Colander: Ideally, the colander should have a pedestal base or feet and secure handles. It is also important that the draining holes are large enough to let water pass quickly, thus keeping the pasta from overcooking while it drains, yet small enough so that not even the smallest pasta can pass through.

Pasta Strainer: This tool is a very pretty, rustic variation on the colander. It has a willow frame and ribs, bamboo binding and a long handle on the end. Pasta is not poured into it as it is with a colander; instead, the strainer is used to scoop and strain pasta directly from the pot. This feature makes it ideal for filled pastas that could be damaged in the transfer from pot to platter, or for medium-size fancy pastas.

Pasta: Fresh and Dry

The choices are exhilarating: Today, supermarket shelves brim with dozens of shapes and brands of domestic and imported dried pasta. And catching up quickly—very quickly—is the array of refrigerated fresh pasta, available seemingly everywhere: supermarkets, department stores, even the corner deli.

Dry pasta should not be considered inferior to the fresh. In fact, it's an excellent product when cooked al dente ("to the tooth") and served with appropriate sauces. It's made from golden semolina flour, which gives it its satisfying, toothsome quality, and is best served with a robust sauce that enhances this hearty texture. It is also excellent for using in cold salads and in baked dishes.

Commercially produced fresh pasta, which is now available all across the country, comes in many different shapes, flavors and colors, and can be used interchangeably with dry in many of the recipes in this book. Although a good product, it does not compare to the homemade version you can prepare, following our directions on the following pages.

The two basic ingredients in homemade pasta are all-purpose white flour and fresh eggs. Other ingredients can be added to enrich its color, flavor and texture. Fresh homemade pasta is neither difficult nor excessively time-consuming to prepare, and the rewards are numerous. This delicate pasta cooks very quickly, and tastes best served with subtle, lightly seasoned sauces.

GETTING READY

It is important to be completely prepared and organized when making fresh pasta. Start by assembling all your ingredients and bringing the eggs and any other refrigerated items to room temperature. If you are mixing the dough by hand, you will need: * large wooden board or marble work surface * a fork for mixing * sieve or strainer * pastry scraper * pastry wheel for cutting * several clean, dry cotton (not terry) kitchen towels. If you are using your food processor, fit it with the plastic blade, and set out a small bowl to beat the eggs.

Ingredients for Fresh Pasta

ALL-PURPOSE WHITE FLOUR is milled from a combination of hard and soft wheat enriched with vitamins and minerals. It is always used for making fresh egg pasta. It produces a very tender dough, which is best cooked when just made or partially dried. White flour is not suitable for commercial dried pasta; rather, this is made from semolina flour, a coarse-textured flour milled from hard durum wheat. Semolina is only rarely used for making fresh pasta, and never used in fresh egg pasta.

WHOLE-WHEAT FLOUR is milled from the entire wheat berry, including the wheat germ and bran, which makes it rich in vitamins, minerals and protein. It is always combined with all-purpose white flour to produce a pasta that is nutty in flavor and texture. Whole-wheat flour has a shorter shelf life than white and should be refrigerated.

BUCKWHEAT FLOUR, ground from the seeds of a low-growing shrub, has no elasticity and therefore must be used with white flour when making pasta. Like whole-wheat flour, it should also be refrigerated.

EGGS should be brought to room temperature when making pasta. Extra large eggs are used in the following recipe, because they absorb about 1 cup of flour, an easy gauge to work by. (Large eggs can be substituted; just use a little less flour.)

OIL is used in many pasta recipes because it produces a smoother dough. Don't add oil to the boiling water when cooking pasta; it creates a greasy coating and prevents pasta from absorbing the sauce. Olive oil is suggested in our recipe for flavor, but corn or safflower oil can be substituted.

SALT is used for flavor in very small amounts in fresh pasta. It is also added to boiling water in cooking pasta so the pasta doesn't "rob" flavor from the sauce. If you prefer not to use it at all, it can be eliminated.

Basic Fresh Pasta Dough

Yield: Approximately 1 pound of pasta dough

1 1/2 - 2 cups all-purpose flour
2 extra-large eggs, at room temperature
2 teaspoons olive oil
1/8 teaspoon salt (optional)

By hand: On work surface, spoon approximately three-quarters of the flour into a mound. Make a well in the center of the flour; break eggs into the well. Add oil and salt. With fork, lightly beat together the liquid ingredients in the well, gradually drawing flour into the well. When the mixture becomes very thick and difficult to mix with the fork, use your hands to form a ball of dough. (At this point, the dough will be wet and sticky.)

Set the ball of dough aside and scrape up all the flour and dough particles stuck to the work surface. Transfer scrapings to the sieve, discarding the dried pieces. Using the sieved flour and the reserved additional flour, resume kneading the dough until smooth and no longer sticky. At this point, the dough is ready for the pasta machine.

Food processor method: Fit processor with plastic blade. Measure 1 1/4 cups flour into workbowl. In a small bowl, lightly beat the eggs, olive oil and salt with a fork; add to the flour. Pulse 5-6 times, just until blended (don't let the mixture form a ball of dough; it should look crumbly). Turn the mixture onto work surface and knead it into a ball, gradually incorporating additional flour, until dough is smooth and no longer sticky.

Kneading and Stretching

Fasten the pasta machine to a sturdy table or
countertop. Adjust the machine to the kneading
position (the first setting on the rotating dial).
Divide the dough into 2 or 3 pieces and work with
one piece at a time (flour the remaining dough,
wrap it in plastic wrap or a clean dry cotton towel,
and set it aside). Flatten the piece of dough, dust it with
flour and feed it into the machine. Flour the bottom only,
fold the dough into thirds like a letter and, using your fingertips or knuckles,
press to seal the dough, pushing out air. Feed into machine, open (narrow)
end first. Repeat folding and feeding 8-10 times, until dough is very smooth
and no longer sticky; do not over-flour the dough.

Next, turn the dial to the number 2 setting. Lightly flour both sides of the dough
(it is not necessary to fold it at this point) and feed it through the machine once;
turn dial to next setting, flour dough if necessary, and feed it through machine.
Continue feeding the dough and advancing the dial. (*Note:* On some
machines, the last setting may tear the dough. If yours begins to shred as you
feed it through, stop and remove it; turn the dial back one notch and pass the
dough through this setting twice.) The dough is now ready to be cut and dried.

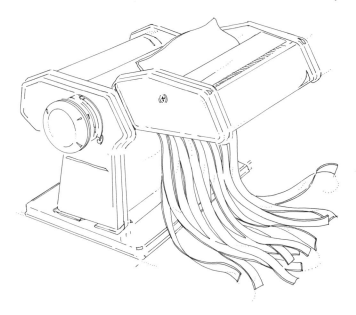

Cutting the Pasta

• *Tagliatelle, fettuccine, spaghetti, linguine and angel hair:* Stretch the dough as thin as possible and cut into 8" strips; arrange side by side on clean dry cotton towels and dry them slightly (do not over-dry, or pasta will become brittle and impossible to cut). Insert desired cutting blade into pasta machine and cut each strip of dough. Lightly flour the cut strands and return them to the towels until ready to use, tossing occasionally.

• *Pappardelle:* Stretch dough as thin as possible; using a fluted pastry wheel, cut into 3/4"-wide strips. Place side by side on towels, flouring lightly if necessary, until ready to use.

• *Lasagna, cannelloni:* Stretch dough as thin as possible; using pastry wheel (straight or fluted), cut into 6" rectangles. Arrange on towels until ready to use. (Fresh lasagna noodles are cut into rectangles, not strips. Rectangles are easier to handle and can be arranged side by side, slightly overlapping, when assembling lasagna.)

• *Bow ties (farfalle):* Stretch dough as thin as possible; using a fluted pastry wheel, cut it into 2x1" rectangles. With thumb and forefinger, pinch the centers of rectangles to form little bows. Arrange on towels until ready to use.

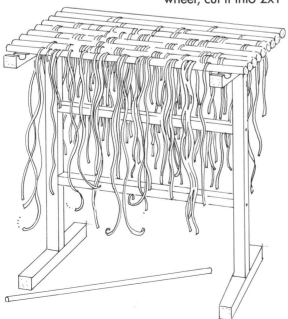

Storing Fresh Pasta

If you are not planning on using the pasta immediately, arrange the cut pasta on clean dry cotton towels, dust lightly with flour and toss from time to time until dry. Store in sealed plastic bags or containers in a cool dry place, or refrigerate 2-3 weeks. Pasta can also be frozen up to one month.

COOKING FRESH AND DRY PASTA
For each pound of pasta, bring 4 quarts of water to a full rolling boil in a large pot. Add the pasta; stir and cover the pot. When the water returns to a boil, uncover, stir and begin timing. For dried commercial pasta, follow the label directions, but begin testing for doneness a few minutes before the end of the suggested cooking time; when done to taste, drain immediately and place in serving bowl. (Never rinse with water unless a recipe specifies to do so, as in chilled pasta salads.) Toss quickly with sauce.

Fresh pasta takes only 10-15 seconds to cook after the water returns to a boil; if it has been dried or frozen, it will take a few minutes longer. Taste for doneness; it should be tender, with no raw floury taste.

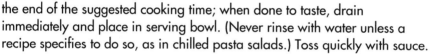

FLAVORED FRESH PASTA
The following different pastas can be made following the directions for Basic Pasta Dough.
Green, Red or Pink Pasta
To basic pasta dough recipe, add 1 heaping tablespoon of drained squeezed chopped spinach, 1 heaping tablespoon tomato paste or 1 heaping tablespoon finely chopped cooked beets.

Whole-Wheat Pasta
Replace one cup of the all-purpose flour with one cup whole-wheat flour.

Fresh Herb Pasta
To basic pasta dough, add any one of the following fresh herbs, or a combination (1 or 2 teaspoons, to taste): parsley, basil, tarragon, thyme, chives or oregano, finely chopped.

Lemon Pasta:
To basic pasta dough, add 1-2 teaspoons finely grated lemon peel.

Soups

Although many will attest that nothing says love better than chicken soup, if you quiz people about this classic comfort food, their main requirement is a bowl filled with lots and lots of noodles. Soups with pasta have always delighted; even a simple tomato soup is more exciting with a few pasta shells afloat. And who could forget a child's glee at finding her name in a bowl of alphabet soup? Besides its reputation as a nourishing, satisfying food, soup offers a low-fat way to enjoy pasta, since broths and vegetables provide the base of many varieties. Keep in mind that smaller shapes of pasta—wagon wheels, stars, bow ties—are easier to eat with a spoon, but thin noodles like angel hair or vermicelli also work well. Colored pastas—spinach, tomato, beet—look wonderful in creamy white soups and clear broths. We couldn't feature soups without including Pasta Fagioli, and we've added some new, soon-to-be standards like Spinach and Shells Soup and Curried Chicken-Corn Soup. Chill out in warm weather with spicy Mexican Gazpacho or creamy Cold Beet-Cucumber Soup, two cold soups topped with hot pasta. Treat your friends to a dinner where Bouillabaisse is the main attraction. Our version, full of seafood and pasta, is great with crusty French bread. Add your own favorite shapes and create a new pasta-soup classic.

26 Tomatillo Soup

Makes 2 servings

Light sour cream gives this soup a creamy consistency and cools off the bite of spicy jalapeño pepper.

1½ teaspoons olive or canola oil
¼ cup chopped onion
1 garlic clove, minced
1½ cups low-sodium chicken broth
8 tomatillos, husked and quartered
1 tablespoon chopped seeded
   jalapeño pepper

1½ ounces tri-color radiatore or
   rotelle, cooked and drained
¼ cup light sour cream
1 tablespoon sliced natural almonds

1. In medium saucepan, heat oil; add onion and garlic. Cook, stirring occasionally, until onion is translucent, about 5 minutes. Add broth, tomatillos and jalapeño pepper; bring to a boil. Reduce heat to medium low; simmer, partially covered, 7 minutes. Remove from heat; cool slightly.

2. In blender or food processor, puree tomatillo mixture, in batches, until smooth; return to saucepan. Add pasta and sour cream; cook just until heated through. Ladle evenly into 4 soup bowls; sprinkle with almonds.

EACH SERVING (1 CUP) PROVIDES: 1 FAT; 1¼ VEGETABLES; 1 BREAD; 90 OPTIONAL CALORIES.
PER SERVING: 301 CALORIES; 12 G PROTEIN; 13 G FAT; 37 G CARBOHYDRATE; 51 MG SODIUM;
10 MG CHOLESTEROL; 2 G DIETARY FIBER.

REDUCED SODIUM AND CHOLESTEROL

Cold Beet-Cucumber Soup with Hot Pasta

Makes 4 servings

This vividly-colored creamy soup is wonderful as the first course to an early spring meal, followed by grilled fish and fresh asparagus.

1 large cucumber, pared, halved
   and seeded
2 cups drained canned julienne-cut
   beets (reserve juice)
1¾ cups low-fat (1%) buttermilk
3 tablespoons snipped fresh dill

2 tablespoons fresh lime juice
½ teaspoon salt
3 ounces spinach penne or mostaccioli
3 tablespoons plain nonfat yogurt
2 tablespoons diced radish

1. Dice two tablespoons cucumber; refrigerate and reserve. Cut remaining cucumber into chunks.

2. In food processor, combine cucumber chunks, beets, beet juice, buttermilk, dill, lime juice and salt; process until smooth. Transfer to large bowl; cover and refrigerate until well chilled.

3. Just before serving, cook pasta following label directions; drain. In small bowl, combine yogurt, the reserved cucumber and the radish. Ladle soup evenly into 4 chilled soup bowls; top evenly with hot pasta and the cucumber-yogurt mixture.

EACH SERVING (ABOUT 1¼ CUPS) PROVIDES: ½ MILK; 1½ VEGETABLES; 1 BREAD.
PER SERVING: 176 CALORIES; 8 G PROTEIN; 1 G FAT; 33 G CARBOHYDRATE; 731 MG SODIUM;
4 MG CHOLESTEROL; 4 G DIETARY FIBER.

REDUCED FAT AND CHOLESTEROL

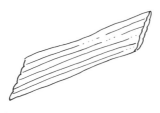

Mexican-Style Gazpacho

Makes 4 servings

This spicy soup is made in the food processor and then chilled. Allow time to cook pasta, which is added to the cold soup just before serving.

1 ½ cups peeled seeded diced plum
   tomatoes
½ cup pared seeded diced cucumber
½ cup diced red onion
½ cup diced green bell pepper
1 garlic clove

2 tablespoons chopped fresh cilantro
2 tablespoons red wine vinegar
2 cups spicy mixed vegetable juice
3 ounces cavatelli or fusilli
Chopped cucumber, red onion and
   bell pepper to garnish

1. In food processor, combine tomatoes, cucumber, onion, bell pepper, garlic, cilantro and vinegar; pulse briefly, just until vegetables are chunky. Pour into large bowl; stir in vegetable juice. Cover and refrigerate until well chilled.

2. Just before serving, cook pasta following label directions; drain. Ladle soup evenly into 4 chilled soup bowls; top evenly with hot pasta. Garnish with chopped vegetables.

EACH SERVING (1 CUP) PROVIDES: 2 VEGETABLES; 1 BREAD.
PER SERVING: 133 CALORIES; 5 G PROTEIN; 1 G FAT; 28 G CARBOHYDRATE; 389 MG SODIUM;
0 MG CHOLESTEROL; 2 G DIETARY FIBER.

REDUCED FAT; CHOLESTEROL-FREE

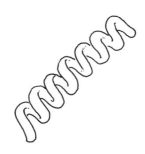

Pasta and Cauliflower Soup

29

Makes 4 servings

Cauliflower and carrot team up with pasta for a new take on your favorite vegetable soup.

2 teaspoons olive oil
½ cup sliced carrot
½ cup finely chopped onion
2 cups cauliflower florets
3 ounces small spinach pasta shells
1 tablespoon chopped fresh basil,
   or 1 teaspoon dried

½ teaspoon salt
1 tablespoon + 1 teaspoon grated
   Romano cheese
Freshly ground black pepper to taste

1. In large saucepan, heat oil. Sauté carrot and onion 5 minutes, until tender, stirring occasionally. Add cauliflower and 4 cups water; cover and cook 5 minutes.

2. Stir in shells, basil and salt; bring to a boil. Cook 12-16 minutes, or until shells are tender. Sprinkle evenly with cheese and pepper.

EACH SERVING PROVIDES: ½ FAT; 1½ VEGETABLES; 1 BREAD; 10 OPTIONAL CALORIES.
PER SERVING: 131 CALORIES; 5 G PROTEIN; 3 G FAT; 22 G CARBOHYDRATE; 313 MG SODIUM;
1 MG CHOLESTEROL; 3 G DIETARY FIBER.

REDUCED FAT AND CHOLESTEROL

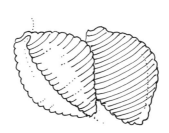

30 Greek Lemon-Pasta Soup

Makes 2 servings

Known as "avgolemono" soup, which means egg and lemon in Greek, this soup is often served at Easter, but feel free to enjoy it anytime.

2 cups low-sodium chicken broth
3 ounces stelline, pastina or small pasta
   rings (anelli)
¼ cup egg substitute

1½ tablespoons fresh lemon juice
⅛ teaspoon salt
1 tablespoon chopped fresh mint

1. In medium saucepan, bring chicken broth to a boil. Add pastina; return to a boil, stirring once. Reduce heat to low; simmer 3-5 minutes. Remove from heat.

2. In small bowl, whisk together egg substitute, lemon juice and salt. Very slowly, whisk in ½ cup of the hot broth. Over very low heat, very slowly drizzle egg mixture into soup in saucepan, stirring constantly; do not let boil, or soup will curdle. Serve immediately, garnished with chopped mint.

EACH SERVING (1 CUP) PROVIDES: ½ PROTEIN; 2 BREADS; 40 OPTIONAL CALORIES.
PER SERVING: 204 CALORIES; 10 G PROTEIN; 2 G FAT; 35 G CARBOHYDRATE; 235 MG SODIUM;
0 MG CHOLESTEROL; 1 G DIETARY FIBER.

REDUCED FAT; CHOLESTEROL-FREE

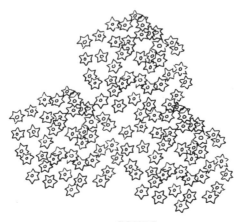

31 **Pistou**

Makes 4 servings

This soup, often found bubbling in French home kitchens, combines pasta, vegetables and beans in a simple, nourishing recipe. You can choose your own favorite vegetables and pasta shapes for variety.

¾ cup sliced carrots
5 ounces diced pared potatoes
½ cup sliced leeks (white part only)
1 large vegetarian vegetable
   bouillon cube
1 cup trimmed green beans,
   cut into 2" pieces
3 ounces whole-wheat vermicelli
4 ounces rinsed drained cooked
   cannellini beans

1 tablespoon tomato paste
¾ ounce grated Romano cheese
1 garlic clove, minced
2 tablespoons finely chopped fresh
   basil
1 tablespoon + 1 teaspoon olive oil

1. In large saucepan, combine carrots, potatoes, leeks, bouillon cube and 6 cups water. Bring to a boil, stirring occasionally. Reduce heat to low; simmer, covered, stirring occasionally, 30 minutes.

2. Add green beans and pasta; stir to combine. Simmer, stirring occasionally, 10 minutes. Stir in cannellini beans.

3. In small bowl, whisk together tomato paste, Romano cheese, garlic and basil. Whisk in oil in a slow, steady stream. Stir ¹/₂ cup of the hot broth into the basil mixture, then gradually stir into soup.

EACH SERVING (ABOUT 1¹/₃ CUPS) PROVIDES: 1 FAT; ³/₄ PROTEIN; 1 VEGETABLE; 1¹/₄ BREADS; 10 OPTIONAL CALORIES.
PER SERVING: 233 CALORIES; 9 G PROTEIN; 7 G FAT; 37 G CARBOHYDRATE; 360 MG SODIUM; 6 MG CHOLESTEROL; 6 G DIETARY FIBER.

REDUCED FAT, SODIUM AND CHOLESTEROL

32 Chinese Noodle-Vegetable Soup

Makes 4 servings

A purely vegetarian dish with snappy Oriental flavor. Tofu cubes provide protein and soak up the spicy soup.

2 teaspoons sesame oil
1 cup broccoflower or broccoli florets
½ cup sliced carrot
2 teaspoons minced ginger root
1 garlic clove, minced
1 large vegetarian vegetable
  bouillon cube

3 ounces udon or bean thread noodles,
  broken into 2" pieces
1 cup shredded bok choy
  (Chinese cabbage)
½ cup trimmed snow peas
8 ounces cubed firm tofu
Hot red pepper sauce to taste

1. In large saucepan, heat oil; add florets, carrot, ginger and garlic. Cook over medium-high heat, stirring frequently, until vegetables are crisp-tender, about 5 minutes.

2. Add bouillon cube, 5 cups water, noodles, bok choy and snow peas; stir to combine. Bring to a boil, stirring occasionally. Reduce heat to low; simmer 10 minutes. Add tofu; cook until heated through. Add hot pepper sauce to taste; serve immediately.

EACH SERVING PROVIDES: ½ FAT; 1 PROTEIN; 1½ VEGETABLES; 1 BREAD; 5 OPTIONAL CALORIES.
PER SERVING: 204 CALORIES; 11 G PROTEIN; 8 G FAT; 26 G CARBOHYDRATE; 282 MG SODIUM;
0 MG CHOLESTEROL; 1 G DIETARY FIBER.

CHOLESTEROL-FREE

Spinach and Shells Soup

Makes 4 servings

Top this soup, brimming with pasta shells and beans, with freshly grated Parmesan cheese, and serve with garlic bread or toasted pita triangles.

1 ½ cups low-sodium chicken broth
1 cup low-sodium stewed tomatoes
4 ½ ounces small pasta shells
14 ounces drained rinsed cannellini beans

1 cup spinach leaves
½ teaspoon dried oregano
½ teaspoon dried basil
¾ ounce grated Parmesan cheese

1. In large saucepan, over medium heat, bring chicken broth to a boil.

2. Add tomatoes and pasta shells; cook 7 minutes. Add beans, spinach, oregano and basil; cook 8-10 minutes, until pasta is tender. (If soup is too thick, thin with a little water.)

3. Ladle evenly into 4 bowls; top evenly with Parmesan cheese.

EACH SERVING PROVIDES: 2 PROTEINS; 1 VEGETABLE; 1 1/2 BREADS; 15 OPTIONAL CALORIES.
PER SERVING: 276 CALORIES; 15 G PROTEIN; 3 G FAT; 48 G CARBOHYDRATE; 294 MG SODIUM;
1 MG CHOLESTEROL; 8 G DIETARY FIBER.

REDUCED FAT, SODIUM AND CHOLESTEROL

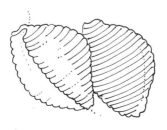

Whole-Wheat Pasta Fagioli

Makes 4 servings

A classic pasta and bean combination. Spaghetti is broken into sections before cooking to make this soup easier to spoon.

2 teaspoons olive oil
1 cup chopped drained canned tomatoes
2 garlic cloves, crushed
½ teaspoon salt
½ teaspoon dried oregano
6 ounces thin whole-wheat spaghetti, broken into 3" pieces

12 ounces drained rinsed cannellini beans
2 tablespoons grated Parmesan cheese
2 tablespoons chopped fresh Italian parsley

1. In medium saucepan, heat oil; sauté tomatoes and garlic 3 minutes, stirring occasionally. Add 3 cups water, the salt and oregano; bring to a boil. Add spaghetti; cook 7 minutes, until almost tender.

2. Stir in beans; cook 3-4 minutes longer, until spaghetti is tender. Sprinkle with Parmesan cheese and parsley.

EACH SERVING PROVIDES: ¹/₂ FAT; 1¹/₂ PROTEINS; ¹/₂ VEGETABLE; 2 BREADS; 15 OPTIONAL CALORIES.
PER SERVING: 295 CALORIES; 15 G PROTEIN; 5 G FAT; 51 G CARBOHYDRATE; 598 MG SODIUM;
2 MG CHOLESTEROL; 11 G DIETARY FIBER.

REDUCED FAT AND CHOLESTEROL

Macaroni Chick-Pea Soup

Makes 4 servings

You'll want to keep your pantry stocked with these basic ingredients so you can make this satisfying soup any time!

2 cups low-sodium chicken broth
3 ounces elbow macaroni
½ teaspoon dried celery flakes
½ teaspoon dried oregano

1 cup low-sodium stewed tomatoes
1 cup cut green beans
2 ounces drained rinsed chick-peas
¼ teaspoon garlic powder

1. In large saucepan, bring broth and 1 cup water to a boil. Reduce heat to low. Add macaroni, celery flakes and oregano; simmer 4 minutes, stirring occasionally.

2. Add stewed tomatoes, green beans, chick-peas and garlic powder, simmer 5 minutes, or until macaroni and beans are tender, stirring occasionally.

EACH SERVING PROVIDES: ¼ PROTEIN; 1 VEGETABLE; 1 BREAD; 20 OPTIONAL CALORIES.
PER SERVING: 137 CALORIES; 6 G PROTEIN; 2 G FAT; 25 G CARBOHYDRATE; 164 MG SODIUM;
0 MG CHOLESTEROL; 2 G DIETARY FIBER.

REDUCED FAT AND SODIUM; CHOLESTEROL-FREE

36 **Winter Vegetable Soup**

Makes 4 servings

Packed with vegetables and fragrant with marjoram, this soup is wonderful to enjoy when nights turn frosty. Serve with toasted rye or pumpernickel bread.

2 teaspoons olive oil
1 cup slivered onion
½ cup sliced carrot
½ cup diced pared parsnip
1 garlic clove, minced
2 large vegetarian vegetable
   bouillon cubes
2 teaspoons dried marjoram

3 ounces penne, mostaccioli or ziti
1 cup trimmed green beans, cut into
   2" lengths
2 cups sliced mushrooms
2 cups finely shredded Swiss chard
1 tablespoon + 1 teaspoon grated
   Parmesan cheese

1. In large saucepan, heat oil; add onion, carrot, parsnip and garlic. Cook over medium-high heat, stirring frequently, until onion is translucent, about 5 minutes.

2. Crumble in bouillon cubes and marjoram. Add 5 cups water; bring to a boil. Add penne and green beans; return to a boil. Reduce heat to low; simmer, partially covered, 15 minutes. Add mushrooms and Swiss chard; simmer 5 minutes longer. Ladle evenly into 4 soup bowls; top evenly with Parmesan cheese.

EACH SERVING (1½ CUPS) PROVIDES: ½ FAT; 3 VEGETABLES; 1¼ BREADS; 20 OPTIONAL CALORIES.
PER SERVING: 171 CALORIES; 6 G PROTEIN; 4 G FAT; 29 G CARBOHYDRATE; 577 MG SODIUM;
1 MG CHOLESTEROL; 3 G DIETARY FIBER.

REDUCED FAT AND CHOLESTEROL

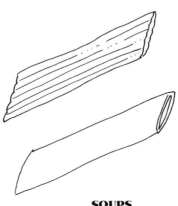

37 **Curried Chicken-Corn Soup**

Makes 4 servings

For a fast supper, you can cook and slice the chicken ahead of time. Serve this soup with a watercress salad and flat Middle Eastern or Indian bread.

4 cups low-sodium chicken broth
½ cup sliced scallions
12 ounces boneless skinless chicken breasts
2 teaspoons corn or canola oil

1 tablespoon curry powder, or to taste
3 ounces fideos or other thin spaghetti
1 cup frozen corn

1. In large nonstick skillet, bring 1 cup of the chicken broth and 1 tablespoon of the scallions to a boil; add chicken breasts. Reduce heat to low; cover and simmer until chicken is cooked through, about 20 minutes. Remove chicken; reserve broth. When chicken is cool enough to handle, cut into bite-sized pieces.

2. In large saucepan, heat oil; add the remaining scallions and the curry powder. Cook over medium-high heat, stirring constantly, 1 minute. Add the reserved cooking liquid, the remaining 3 cups chicken broth, the pasta and corn; bring to a boil. Reduce heat to low; simmer 5 minutes, until pasta is tender. Add chicken; heat through.

EACH SERVING (1¼ CUPS) PROVIDES: ½ FAT; 2 PROTEINS; ¼ VEGETABLE; 1½ BREADS; 40 OPTIONAL CALORIES.
PER SERVING: 268 CALORIES; 26 G PROTEIN; 6 G FAT; 28 G CARBOHYDRATE; 114 MG SODIUM; 49 MG CHOLESTEROL; 2 G DIETARY FIBER.

REDUCED FAT, SODIUM AND CHOLESTEROL

38 Turkey Soup with Pasta

Makes 4 servings

Turkey leftovers from Thanksgiving can be put to great use in this soup.

1 tablespoon + 1 teaspoon reduced-calorie tub margarine
2 cups diced carrots
2 cups diced onions
1 tablespoon + 1 teaspoon all-purpose flour
Pinch freshly ground black pepper

4 packets low-sodium chicken broth mix
2 teaspoons dried basil
8 ounces shredded cooked turkey
3 ounces small pasta shells
½ teaspoon salt
Pinch ground red pepper

1. In large saucepan, melt margarine; add carrots and onions. Cook, stirring frequently, 4-5 minutes, until just tender. Stir in flour and black pepper; cook 1 minute longer. Stir in 6 cups water, the broth mix and basil; bring to a boil.

2. Reduce heat to low; stir in turkey, pasta, salt and red pepper. Cook, stirring frequently, until pasta is cooked and soup is slightly thickened, about 10 minutes.

EACH SERVING PROVIDES: ½ FAT; 2 PROTEINS; 2 VEGETABLES; 1 BREAD; 20 OPTIONAL CALORIES.
PER SERVING: 265 CALORIES; 22 G PROTEIN; 5 G FAT; 32 G CARBOHYDRATE; 376 MG SODIUM;
44 MG CHOLESTEROL; 4 G DIETARY FIBER.

REDUCED FAT, SODIUM AND CHOLESTEROL

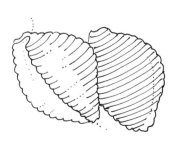

39 Albondigas (Meatball) Soup

Makes 4 servings

The meatballs in this soup are made from lean ground beef and poultry. They get an unexpected zing from fresh cilantro.

4 ounces ground turkey or chicken
4 ounces lean ground beef
½ cup finely chopped onion
2 tablespoons minced fresh cilantro
2 cups low-sodium chicken broth
2 cups low-sodium beef broth

½ teaspoon dried oregano
½ cup slivered carrot
3 ounces ditalini, small bow ties or other small pasta
1 cup fresh spinach leaves, slivered

1. Preheat broiler. Spray broiler rack with nonstick cooking spray.

2. In medium bowl, with fork, lightly combine turkey, beef, 1 tablespoon each of the onion and cilantro and 2 tablespoons water; do not overmix. Shape into 16 meatballs. Broil on rack in pan 4" from heat, 10 minutes.

3. In medium saucepan, combine chicken and beef broth, the remaining onion and cilantro, the oregano and meatballs. Bring to a boil, stirring occasionally. Add carrot and pasta; stir to combine. Return to a boil; reduce heat to medium-low and simmer, stirring occasionally, until pasta and carrot are tender, about 10 minutes. Add spinach; stir to combine. Simmer 5 minutes longer.

EACH SERVING (1 CUP) PROVIDES: 1½ PROTEINS; 1 VEGETABLE; 1 BREAD; 40 OPTIONAL CALORIES.
PER SERVING: 227 CALORIES; 16 G PROTEIN; 9 G FAT; 21 G CARBOHYDRATE; 82 MG SODIUM;
33 MG CHOLESTEROL; 2 G DIETARY FIBER.

REDUCED FAT AND SODIUM

Bouillabaisse

40

Makes 4 servings

This one-dish meal is just perfect served in large bowls to give diners room to scoop up the chunks of seafood and pasta. Serve with a mixed green salad dressed lightly with vinaigrette.

2 teaspoons olive oil
½ cup chopped onion
1 garlic clove, minced
2 cups no-salt-added tomatoes
½ cup dry white wine
1 tablespoon chopped fresh parsley
1 tablespoon tomato paste
½ teaspoon dried thyme
1 bay leaf
⅛ teaspoon crushed saffron
   or turmeric

⅛ teaspoon fennel seeds
10 ounces firm white fish
   (cod, haddock or sole),
   cut into 1½" chunks
Two 6-ounce fresh or thawed frozen
   lobster tails, quartered
12 littleneck clams, scrubbed
3 ounces orzo, cooked and drained

1. In large saucepan, heat oil; add onion and garlic. Cook over medium-high heat, stirring occasionally, 3 minutes. Add tomatoes, 1 1/2 cups water, wine, parsley, tomato paste, thyme, bay leaf, saffron and fennel seeds; stir to combine. Bring to a boil, stirring occasionally.

2. Add fish, lobster and clams; return to a boil. Reduce heat to low; simmer, covered, 6-8 minutes, until clams open and fish and lobster are cooked through. (Discard any clams that do not open.) Remove bay leaf.

3. To serve, spoon orzo evenly into 4 shallow soup bowls; ladle bouillabaisse evenly over orzo.

EACH SERVING (ABOUT 1³/4 CUPS) PROVIDES: ¹/2 FAT; 2¹/2 PROTEINS; 1¹/4 VEGETABLES; 1 BREAD; 35 OPTIONAL CALORIES.
PER SERVING: 278 CALORIES; 29 G PROTEIN; 4 G FAT; 26 G CARBOHYDRATE; 268 MG SODIUM; 71 MG CHOLESTEROL; 2 G DIETARY FIBER.

REDUCED FAT AND SODIUM

Baked Pasta

Picture melted strands of mozzarella, tomato sauce fragrant with oregano and basil, mellow ricotta cheese—and you'll understand why baking is one of the preferred ways to prepare pasta. Because it can be cooked in advance, it's ideal for entertaining, and by choosing a baked main course, you leave yourself time to make the rest of your meal extra special. Dried pastas work well in these recipes, since they are sturdy enough to endure the double-cooking process of boiling and baking. Many of the dishes in this chapter can be prepared ahead of time, refrigerated and then baked just before serving, giving you time to entertain guests and serve a first course. Before you bring out Mostaccioli with Spiced Veal Sauce or Chicken Tetrazzini Amandine, why not offer a combination of your favorite *antipasto*? Stuffed mushrooms, celery and fennel stalks, roasted red peppers, slices of fresh mozzarella with fresh basil and just a tiny drizzle of good olive oil are fine starters. Of course, a simple plate of melon and prosciutto is always a classic. Serve cubes of feta, stuffed grape leaves and Calamata olives to set the stage for Pastitsio, a delicious Greek meat and pasta combination with a creamy topping. Try Lamb Pinwheels with Lemon Sauce for an elegant Easter meal. Not just for entertaining, baked dishes like classic Macaroni and Cheese or Spaghetti Pie, a new twist on pizza, are perfect no-fuss meals destined to become family favorites.

42 **Penne with Artichokes**

Makes 4 servings

Just a little dry white wine added to these delicate vegetables and herbs infuses them with full-bodied flavor. Try serving this dish with sliced ripe tomatoes.

1 tablespoon + 1 teaspoon canola oil
1 tablespoon finely chopped onion
1 garlic clove, finely chopped
2 cups thawed frozen artichoke hearts (one 10-ounce package), quartered
2 teaspoons chopped fresh mint
2 teaspoons chopped fresh flat-leaf parsley

Salt and freshly ground black pepper to taste
¼ cup dry white wine
2 tablespoons all-purpose flour
1 cup chicken broth
6 ounces penne, cooked and drained
2 tablespoons freshly grated Parmesan cheese

1. Preheat oven to 425°F. Spray an 8" square baking pan with nonstick cooking spray.

2. In large nonstick skillet, heat oil; add onion and garlic. Sauté, stirring, until onion is translucent, 3 minutes. Add artichoke hearts, parsley, mint, salt and pepper. Increase heat to medium; sauté, stirring constantly, 3 minutes.

3. Add wine; increase heat to high and cook until wine evaporates. Lower heat to medium; sprinkle in flour. Sauté, stirring, 1 minute. Gradually stir in broth; cook, stirring, until thickened and creamy. Remove from heat.

4. Add pasta and 1 tablespoon of the Parmesan cheese to artichoke mixture; toss gently to combine. Transfer to prepared pan; sprinkle evenly with remaining Parmesan. Bake 10-12 minutes; place under broiler to brown top lightly, 1-2 minutes.

EACH SERVING PROVIDES: 1 FAT; 1 VEGETABLE; 2 BREADS; 55 OPTIONAL CALORIES.
PER SERVING: 274 CALORIES; 10 G PROTEIN; 7 G FAT; 41 G CARBOHYDRATE; 341 MG SODIUM;
2 MG CHOLESTEROL; 4 G DIETARY FIBER.

REDUCED FAT AND CHOLESTEROL

BAKED PASTA
Slim Ways with Pasta

43 Farfalle with Zucchini and Mint

Makes 4 servings

Celebrate spring with this baked "primavera" featuring fresh mint and tender squash.

1 tablespoon + 1 teaspoon extra virgin olive oil
2 tablespoons finely chopped onion
1 garlic clove, finely chopped
1½ cups canned crushed Italian tomatoes
Salt and freshly ground black pepper to taste

6 ounces farfalle (bow tie pasta), cooked and drained
2 teaspoons chopped fresh mint
1½ cups thinly sliced zucchini
1½ cups thinly sliced yellow squash
3 ounces part-skim mozzarella cheese, finely diced or shredded
2 teaspoons grated Parmesan cheese

1. Preheat oven to 350°F. Spray an 8" square baking pan with nonstick cooking spray.

2. In large saucepan, heat 2 teaspoons of the oil; add onion. Sauté until translucent, 2 minutes. Add garlic; sauté 1 minute. Add tomatoes, salt and pepper to taste; simmer 15 minutes. Stir in pasta and mint; remove from heat.

3. In large nonstick skillet, heat the remaining 2 teaspoons oil; add zucchini and yellow squash. Sauté, stirring occasionally, until golden and slightly wilted, 5 minutes.

4. Spoon half the pasta mixture into prepared pan. Layer with half the squash, then half the mozzarella. Repeat layering with remaining pasta, squash and mozzarella. Sprinkle evenly with Parmesan cheese. Bake 15 minutes, then place under broiler to lightly brown the top, 1-2 minutes.

EACH SERVING PROVIDES: 1 FAT; 1 PROTEIN; 2¼ VEGETABLES; 2 BREADS; 5 OPTIONAL CALORIES.
PER SERVING: 294 CALORIES; 13 G PROTEIN; 10 G FAT; 40 G CARBOHYDRATE; 267 MG SODIUM; 13 MG CHOLESTEROL; 3 G DIETARY FIBER.

REDUCED CHOLESTEROL

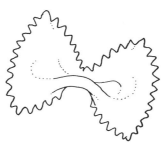

BAKED PASTA
Slim Ways with Pasta

44 Noodles with Mushrooms

Makes 4 servings

Porcini or other wild mushrooms are best suited to this dish, a substantial main course when paired with a salad, or a delightful accompaniment to grilled fish.

½ ounce dried porcini mushrooms
2 teaspoons canola oil
1 tablespoon finely chopped onion
1 garlic clove, finely chopped
2 tablespoons dry white wine
½ cup canned tomatoes, crushed
4 cups sliced fresh mushrooms
Salt and freshly ground black pepper
  to taste

2 teaspoons chopped fresh flat-leaf
  parsley
6 ounces wide noodles, cooked and
  drained
Bechamel Sauce (recipe follows)
2 tablespoons grated Parmesan cheese

1. Preheat oven to 350°F. Spray an 8" square baking pan with nonstick cooking spray.

2. Soak dried mushrooms in ³/₄ cup hot water 30 minutes. Strain liquid through a white paper towel or very fine sieve; reserve liquid. Rinse mushrooms carefully, removing any grit or hard spots. Chop mushrooms coarsely.

3. In medium saucepan, heat oil; add onion and garlic. Sauté, stirring, until onion is translucent, 2 minutes. Add chopped mushrooms; sauté 1 minute. Add wine and tomatoes; cook 3 minutes. Add fresh mushrooms and salt and pepper to taste; cook 5 minutes longer, until mushrooms are tender. Add reserved porcini liquid and parsley; increase heat to medium-high and cook, stirring occasionally, until mixture thickens. Stir in noodles, prepared Bechamel Sauce and 1 tablespoon of the Parmesan cheese.

4. Transfer noodle mixture to prepared pan; sprinkle with remaining 1 tablespoon Parmesan cheese. Bake 8-10 minutes, until top is lightly browned.

EACH SERVING PROVIDES: ¼ MILK; 1½ FATS; 2½ VEGETABLES; 2 BREADS; 30 OPTIONAL CALORIES.
PER SERVING: 308 CALORIES; 12 G PROTEIN; 10 G FAT; 43 G CARBOHYDRATE; 227 MG SODIUM;
45 MG CHOLESTEROL; 2 G DIETARY FIBER.

BECHAMEL SAUCE:
In heavy medium saucepan, melt 1 tablespoon + 1 teaspoon margarine; whisk in 1 tablespoon + 1 teaspoon all-purpose flour; cook, whisking constantly, 1 minute. Gradually whisk in 1 cup low-fat (1%) milk and pinch each salt, white pepper and ground nutmeg. Bring to a boil, whisking constantly; lower heat and cook 1 minute. Remove from heat; whisk before using.

45 Whole-Wheat Tagliatelle with Swiss Chard

Makes 4 servings

Since this dish bakes for just 10 minutes, you can prepare it ahead of time and refrigerate, baking it just before serving.

2 teaspoons canola oil
2 tablespoons finely chopped onion
2 cloves garlic, finely chopped
1 tablespoon chopped fresh sage
1 cup trimmed green beans, cut into 2" pieces
6 cups sliced Swiss chard

6 ounces whole-wheat tagliatelle, cooked and drained
Salt and freshly ground black pepper to taste
3 ounces Italian Fontina cheese, shredded
1 tablespoon grated Parmesan cheese

1. In medium saucepan, combine oil, onion, garlic, sage and 1 tablespoon water; cook over medium heat until water evaporates, 5 minutes. Lower heat and cook, stirring occasionally, until onion is golden. Set aside.

2. Preheat oven to 350°F. Spray an 8" square baking pan with nonstick cooking spray.

3. In large pot of boiling water, cook green beans until almost tender, 3-4 minutes. Add Swiss chard and cook 3-4 minutes longer, until tender. Drain in colander, pressing lightly to extract excess water. Set aside.

4. Place pasta in large bowl; toss with onion mixture, vegetables, salt and pepper to taste. Spoon half the pasta mixture into prepared pan; sprinkle with half the Fontina and Parmesan cheese. Repeat layering. Cover and bake 10 minutes, until hot and bubbly.

EACH SERVING PROVIDES: 1/2 FAT; 1 PROTEIN; 3 1/2 VEGETABLES; 2 BREADS; 10 OPTIONAL CALORIES.
PER SERVING: 280 CALORIES; 14 G PROTEIN; 10 G FAT; 37 G CARBOHYDRATE; 314 MG SODIUM;
26 MG CHOLESTEROL; 6 G DIETARY FIBER.

BAKED PASTA
Slim Ways with Pasta

46 **Baked Ziti with Red Pepper Bechamel**

Makes 4 servings

Ziti, which means "bridegrooms" in Italian, stands up well in zesty dishes like this one. Serve a side dish of broccoli sautéed with garlic.

2 teaspoons canola oil
1 large red bell pepper, thinly sliced
½ cup finely chopped red onion
1 garlic clove, finely chopped
¼ cup canned Italian tomatoes, crushed
1 small sprig fresh rosemary

Pinch dried red pepper flakes
Bechamel Sauce (recipe follows)
6 ounces ziti, cooked and drained
2 tablespoons grated Parmesan cheese
1 tablespoon chopped fresh flat-leaf parsley

1. Preheat oven to 375°F. Spray an 8" square baking pan with nonstick cooking spray.

2. In medium nonstick skillet, heat oil; add pepper. Sauté, stirring, 3 minutes, until just tender. Add onion and garlic; sauté 2 minutes, until onion is softened.

3. Add tomatoes, ½ cup water, rosemary and pepper flakes; cover and simmer until peppers are completely soft, 20 minutes. Uncover and cook until any remaining liquid evaporates.

4. Press mixture through medium disk of a food mill (or through a wire mesh sieve). Transfer to large bowl; stir in Bechamel Sauce. Add pasta and 1 tablespoon of the Parmesan cheese; toss to combine.

5. Scrape mixture into prepared pan; sprinkle with the remaining 1 tablespoon Parmesan cheese. Bake 15 minutes; sprinkle with parsley.

EACH SERVING PROVIDES: ¼ MILK; 1½ FATS; 1½ VEGETABLES; 2 BREADS; 25 OPTIONAL CALORIES.
PER SERVING: 283 CALORIES; 10 G PROTEIN; 8 G FAT; 42 G CARBOHYDRATE; 185 MG SODIUM;
4 MG CHOLESTEROL; 2 G DIETARY FIBER.

REDUCED FAT, SODIUM AND CHOLESTEROL

BECHAMEL SAUCE:
In heavy medium saucepan, melt 1 tablespoon + 1 teaspoon margarine; whisk in 1 tablespoon + 1 teaspoon all-purpose flour; cook, whisking constantly, 1 minute. Gradually whisk in 1 cup low-fat (1%) milk and pinch each salt, white pepper and ground nutmeg. Bring to a boil, whisking constantly; lower heat and cook 1 minute. Remove from heat; whisk before using.

Baked Radiatore with Pesto Bechamel

47

Makes 4 servings

This creamy basil-flavored sauce nestles inside all the grooves of this curvy pasta. Topped with pignolias and bread crumbs, it's a great dish to bring visiting.

3 cups basil leaves
2 garlic cloves, finely chopped
Bechamel Sauce (recipe follows)
6 ounces radiatore, cooked and drained
2 tablespoons grated Parmesan cheese

2 tablespoons + 2 teaspoons pignolias (pine nuts)
1 tablespoon + 1 teaspoon dried bread crumbs

1. Preheat oven to 365°F. Spray an 8" square baking pan with nonstick cooking spray.

2. In food processor, puree basil and garlic until coarsely chopped. Add Bechamel Sauce, scraping sides of work bowl; process until blended. Scrape into medium bowl; stir in pasta, 1 tablespoon of the Parmesan cheese and the pignolias.

3. Sprinkle prepared pan with 2 teaspoons of the bread crumbs. Scrape pasta into pan; sprinkle evenly with the remaining bread crumbs and Parmesan cheese.

4. Bake 15 minutes, then place under broiler to lightly brown.

EACH SERVING PROVIDES: 1/4 MILK; 1 1/2 FATS; 1/4 PROTEIN; 2 BREADS; 35 OPTIONAL CALORIES.
PER SERVING: 300 CALORIES; 12 G PROTEIN; 8 G FAT; 47 G CARBOHYDRATE; 178 MG SODIUM;
5 MG CHOLESTEROL; 1 G DIETARY FIBER.

REDUCED FAT, SODIUM AND CHOLESTEROL

BECHAMEL SAUCE:
In heavy medium saucepan, melt 1 tablespoon + 1 teaspoon margarine; whisk in 1 tablespoon + 1 teaspoon all-purpose flour; cook, whisking constantly, 1 minute. Gradually whisk in 1 cup low-fat (1%) milk and pinch each salt, white pepper and ground nutmeg. Bring to a boil, whisking constantly; lower heat and cook 1 minute. Remove from heat; whisk before using.

48 Herbed Gnocchi with Tomato-Onion Sauce

Makes 4 servings

Here's a basic recipe for homemade gnocchi and a great sauce.

½ cup canned Italian tomatoes, crushed
½ cup finely chopped onion
2 teaspoons margarine
Pinch sugar
Salt and freshly ground black pepper to taste
15 ounces white boiling potatoes, scrubbed, unpared

½ cup plus 2 tablespoons all-purpose flour
½ teaspoon finely chopped fresh rosemary
½ teaspoon finely chopped fresh sage
2 tablespoons grated Parmesan cheese

1. To prepare sauce, in medium saucepan, combine tomatoes, onion, margarine, sugar, salt and pepper to taste. Bring to a boil; lower heat and simmer 30 minutes. Transfer to food processor; puree until smooth.

2. To prepare gnocchi, in another medium saucepan, boil potatoes in water to cover until just tender when pierced with knife. Let drain until cool enough to handle. Peel potatoes and press through medium disk of a food mill or a potato ricer into a large bowl.

3. Add ¹/2 cup of the flour, the herbs and black pepper to taste; combine thoroughly with potatoes. Sprinkle work surface with the remaining 2 tablespoons flour; turn potato mixture out of bowl onto surface and knead until smooth but slightly sticky. Divide into 4 equal pieces. Roll one piece at a time into a ³/4" cylinder; cut into ³/4" lengths. (Keep gnocchi separated as they are cut.)

4. Preheat oven to 375°F. Spray a 9" square baking pan with nonstick cooking spray. Spread a thin layer of the tomato-onion sauce in prepared pan.

5. In large pot of boiling water, cook gnocchi in batches without crowding, for about 10 seconds, stirring gently, until gnocchi float to surface. Remove with a slotted spoon to a single layer in prepared pan. Repeat until all gnocchi are cooked. Cover with remaining tomato sauce. Sprinkle with Parmesan cheese and bake 7 minutes, then place under broiler to lightly brown.

EACH SERVING PROVIDES: ¹/2 FAT; ¹/2 VEGETABLE; 1¹/2 BREADS; 25 OPTIONAL CALORIES.

PER SERVING: 198 CALORIES; 6 G PROTEIN; 3 G FAT; 37 G CARBOHYDRATE; 125 MG SODIUM; 2 MG CHOLESTEROL; 3 G DIETARY FIBER.

REDUCED FAT, SODIUM AND CHOLESTEROL

49 Rotelle with Mozzarella and Olives

Makes 4 servings

Be sure to use imported Gaeta or Calamata olives—their assertive taste brings a lot of flavor to this dish. They're available in many supermarkets.

1 tablespoon extra virgin olive oil
1 tablespoon finely chopped onion
1 tablespoon finely chopped carrot
1 tablespoon finely chopped celery
1½ teaspoons finely chopped garlic
Pinch salt
1½ cups canned Italian whole tomatoes

2 tablespoons chopped fresh basil
Freshly ground black pepper to taste
6 ounces rotelle, cooked and drained
½ teaspoon dried oregano
10 small Calamata olives, pitted and chopped
3 ounces shredded part-skim mozzarella cheese

1. Preheat oven to 375°F. Spray an 8" square baking pan with nonstick cooking spray.

2. In medium saucepan, heat oil; add onion, carrot, celery, garlic and salt. Sauté over medium-low heat, stirring, 5 minutes.

3. Add tomatoes, crushing with back of spoon; stir in 1 tablespoon of the basil and the black pepper; cook, stirring occasionally, 20 minutes. Stir in pasta, the remaining 1 tablespoon basil, the oregano and olives.

4. Spoon pasta mixture into prepared pan; sprinkle evenly with mozzarella. Cover and bake 10 minutes.

EACH SERVING PROVIDES: 1 FAT; 1 PROTEIN; 3/4 VEGETABLE; 2 BREADS.
PER SERVING: 291 CALORIES; 12 G PROTEIN; 11 G FAT; 38 G CARBOHYDRATE; 517 MG SODIUM;
12 MG CHOLESTEROL; 2 G DIETARY FIBER.

REDUCED CHOLESTEROL

BAKED PASTA
Slim Ways with Pasta

50 Shells with Spinach and Ricotta

Makes 4 servings

Spinach, an excellent source of vitamin A, calcium and potassium, makes this pasta standard more nutritious and colorful. Serve with a side dish of marinated roasted red peppers.

2 teaspoons canola oil
2 tablespoons finely chopped onion
2 cups drained thawed frozen chopped spinach (one 10-ounce package)
½ cup chicken broth
Salt and freshly ground black pepper to taste

1 cup part-skim ricotta cheese
½ cup low-fat (2%) milk
Dash freshly grated nutmeg
2 tablespoons grated Parmesan cheese
6 ounces medium pasta shells, cooked and drained

1. Preheat oven to 425°F. Spray an 8" square baking pan with nonstick cooking spray.

2. In large nonstick skillet, heat oil; add onion. Sauté, stirring, until onion is translucent, 2 minutes. Add spinach; sauté 2 minutes, stirring. Add broth and salt and pepper to taste; cook 2 minutes longer. Transfer to large bowl.

3. Add ricotta and milk to spinach mixture; stir to combine. Add nutmeg, 1 tablespoon of the Parmesan and the pasta shells; mix thoroughly.

4. Transfer mixture to prepared pan; sprinkle evenly with the remaining 1 tablespoon Parmesan. Bake 10 minutes, then place under broiler to brown lightly.

EACH SERVING PROVIDES: ½ FAT; 1 PROTEIN; 1 VEGETABLE; 2 BREADS; 35 OPTIONAL CALORIES.
PER SERVING: 314 CALORIES; 17 G PROTEIN; 10 G FAT; 40 G CARBOHYDRATE; 318 MG SODIUM; 23 MG CHOLESTEROL; 3 G DIETARY FIBER.

REDUCED FAT AND CHOLESTEROL

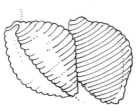

BAKED PASTA
Slim Ways with Pasta

51 Baked Shells with Eggplant and Cheese

Makes 4 servings

Cheesy with provolone and ricotta, this simple baked dish is inspired by some basic ingredients of Italian cooking. A tray of sliced fennel and celery sticks, some roasted peppers and a bowl of assorted olives are wonderful accompaniments.

2 teaspoons olive oil
1 tablespoon finely chopped onion
1 garlic clove, finely chopped
2 cups trimmed diced Italian eggplant
Salt to taste
2 cups canned Italian plum
  tomatoes, crushed

1 ½ teaspoons chopped fresh
  mint or basil
6 ounces medium pasta shells, cooked
  and drained
1 ½ ounces grated provolone cheese
½ cup part-skim ricotta cheese

1. Preheat oven to 400°F. Spray an 8" square baking pan with nonstick cooking spray.

2. In large saucepan, heat oil; add onion and garlic. Sauté, stirring, until onion is translucent, 2 minutes. Add eggplant and a pinch of salt; sauté, stirring, until eggplant is tender, about 10 minutes.

3. Add tomatoes and mint; cover and simmer, stirring occasionally, 25 minutes. Stir in pasta, provolone and ricotta cheese; toss to combine.

4. Transfer mixture to prepared pan; bake 12 minutes.

EACH SERVING PROVIDES: ¹/₂ FAT; 1 PROTEIN; 2 VEGETABLES; 2 BREADS.
PER SERVING: 294 CALORIES; 13 G PROTEIN; 9 G FAT; 42 G CARBOHYDRATE; 332 MG SODIUM;
17 MG CHOLESTEROL; 3 G DIETARY FIBER.

REDUCED FAT AND CHOLESTEROL

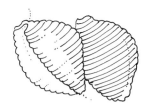

BAKED PASTA
Slim Ways with Pasta

Makes 4 servings

Reminiscent of broccoli and cheese stuffed potatoes, this two-step recipe is healthy fast-food made at home.

4½ ounces ridged or plain elbow macaroni
2 cups cooked broccoli florets
6 ounces reduced-fat cheddar-flavor cheese, cut into ¼" cubes

2 tablespoons plain wheat germ
1 tablespoon imitation bacon bits
1 cup evaporated skimmed milk

1. Preheat oven to 450°F. In large pot of rapidly boiling water, cook macaroni 8-10 minutes, until tender; drain. Return to same pot and combine with remaining ingredients except milk.

2. Spoon mixture into a 6-cup baking dish; pour milk evenly over the top. Bake 12-15 minutes, until golden and bubbly.

EACH SERVING PROVIDES: ½ MILK; 2 PROTEINS; 1 VEGETABLE; 1½ BREADS; 25 OPTIONAL CALORIES.
PER SERVING: 281 CALORIES; 22 G PROTEIN; 4 G FAT; 38 G CARBOHYDRATE; 708 MG SODIUM;
10 MG CHOLESTEROL; 1 G DIETARY FIBER.

REDUCED FAT AND CHOLESTEROL

53 Macaroni and Cheese

Makes 4 servings

Cooking from scratch has never been easier! With just 5 ingredients, this homey casserole can be ready in half an hour.

4½ ounces elbow macaroni
6 ounces processed American cheese, cut into ½" cubes
1 cup skim milk

1 tablespoon + 1 teaspoon margarine
¼ teaspoon freshly ground black pepper

1. Preheat oven to 450°F. Spray a 4-cup baking dish with nonstick cooking spray; set aside.

2. In large pot of rapidly boiling water, cook macaroni 8-10 minutes, until tender; drain.

3. Return macaroni to same pot and combine with remaining ingredients. Spoon mixture into prepared dish; bake 15-18 minutes, until golden and bubbly. Let stand 5 minutes before serving.

EACH SERVING PROVIDES: ¼ MILK; 1 FAT; 2 PROTEINS; 1½ BREADS.
PER SERVING: 335 CALORIES; 16 G PROTEIN; 18 G FAT; 28 G CARBOHYDRATE; 687 MG SODIUM; 41 MG CHOLESTEROL; 1 G DIETARY FIBER.

REDUCED CHOLESTEROL

Pastitsio

54

Makes 4 servings

We've lightened up this classic Greek dish, but the layers of vegetables, ground chicken, tomatoes, spices and creamy tofu topping can't be beat. Serve with "horta"—a salad of wild greens.

FILLING:
2 cups thinly sliced fresh mushrooms
1½ cups coarsely chopped zucchini
1 cup chopped onion
1½ teaspoons dried oregano
¼ teaspoon ground cinnamon
¾ teaspoon salt (optional)
1½ cups low-sodium
   canned tomatoes
8 ounces ground chicken breast
3 ounces elbow macaroni, cooked
   and drained

TOPPING:
9 ounces soft tofu
2 tablespoons plain lowfat yogurt
1 large egg
¼ teaspoon ground cinnamon
¼ teaspoon dry mustard
¼ teaspoon salt (optional)
2 tablespoons grated Parmesan
   cheese

1. In large nonstick skillet, over medium-high heat, cook mushrooms, zucchini, onion, oregano, cinnamon and salt, if using, stirring occasionally, 8 minutes. Add tomatoes, breaking up with a spoon; cook 5 minutes longer. Add ground chicken, stirring to break up; cook 7 minutes longer, or until chicken is opaque and most of the liquid has evaporated.

2. Preheat oven to 375°F.

3. Spray a 9" square baking pan with nonstick cooking spray; spoon macaroni into pan. Top evenly with chicken-vegetable mixture. Cover with foil; bake 20 minutes.

4. Meanwhile, to prepare topping, in food processor, combine tofu, yogurt, egg, cinnamon, mustard and salt, if using; process until smooth, about 1 minute.

5. Remove foil from pastitsio. Spoon topping evenly over mixture and sprinkle with Parmesan cheese. Return pan to oven and bake 15-20 minutes longer, or until set.

EACH SERVING PROVIDES: 2½ PROTEINS; 3 VEGETABLES; 1 BREAD; 20 OPTIONAL CALORIES.
PER SERVING: 282 CALORIES; 25 G PROTEIN; 6 G FAT; 33 G CARBOHYDRATE; 125 MG SODIUM;
88 MG CHOLESTEROL; 3 G DIETARY FIBER.

REDUCED FAT AND SODIUM

55 Pasta Brunch Bake

Makes 4 servings

Although they share similar ingredients, this dish is a simple, tasty change from the typical brunch or luncheon quiche.

1 ½ ounces elbow macaroni,
  cooked and drained
1 cup chopped cooked broccoli
½ cup drained canned sliced
  mushrooms
6 ounces shredded cheddar cheese
3 ounces chopped cooked turkey ham
1 cup evaporated skimmed milk

¼ cup egg substitute
1 tablespoon Dijon mustard
¼ teaspoon freshly ground black
  pepper
2 teaspoons reduced-calorie tub
  margarine, melted
⅛ teaspoon paprika

1. Preheat oven to 350°F. Spray an 8" square baking pan with nonstick cooking spray.

2. In medium bowl, combine macaroni, broccoli, mushrooms, 4 ounces of the cheese and the turkey ham. Spoon into prepared pan, patting down with back of wooden spoon. In a small bowl, stir together milk, egg substitute, mustard and pepper; pour over macaroni mixture. Sprinkle remaining 2 ounces cheese over top.

3. Drizzle margarine evenly over cheese; sprinkle with paprika. Bake 20 minutes, or until golden. Let stand 5 minutes before serving. Serve hot or chilled.

EACH SERVING PROVIDES: 1/2 MILK; 1/4 FAT; 3 PROTEINS; 3/4 VEGETABLE; 1/2 BREAD.
PER SERVING: 335 CALORIES; 24 G PROTEIN; 17 G FAT; 22 G CARBOHYDRATE; 781 MG SODIUM;
60 MG CHOLESTEROL; 2 G DIETARY FIBER.

BAKED PASTA
Slim Ways with Pasta

56 Chicken Tetrazzini Amandine

Makes 6 servings

A popular classic you can plan ahead for the next time you roast a chicken. Serve this tasty dish with a colorful salad of arugula, radicchio and endive.

1 tablespoon + 1 teaspoon
  reduced-calorie tub margarine
1 ½ cups thinly sliced mushrooms
2 tablespoons all-purpose flour
1 ½ cups evaporated skimmed milk
½ cup low-sodium chicken broth

1 ounce toasted slivered almonds
½ teaspoon dried basil
6 ¾ ounces spaghetti, cooked
  and drained
8 ounces cubed cooked chicken breast
1 tablespoon grated Parmesan cheese

1. Preheat oven to 350°F. Spray an 11x7" baking pan with nonstick cooking spray.

2. To prepare mushroom sauce, in small saucepan, melt margarine; add mushrooms. Cook, stirring frequently, 2 minutes. Stir in flour; cook 1 minute, stirring constantly. Pour in ½ cup of the milk, the broth and ½ cup water. Stir until blended. Cook 2-3 minutes, stirring, until thickened. Remove from heat; stir in the remaining 1 cup milk, the almonds and basil.

3. Place spaghetti in prepared pan; top with chicken. Pour mushroom sauce over chicken; sprinkle with cheese.

4. Bake 20-25 minutes, until lightly browned and bubbly. Let cool 5 minutes before serving.

EACH SERVING PROVIDES: ½ MILK; ¾ FAT; 1½ PROTEINS; ½ VEGETABLE; 1½ BREADS; 20 OPTIONAL CALORIES.
PER SERVING: 295 CALORIES, 23 G PROTEIN; 7 G FAT; 35 G CARBOHYDRATE; 151 MG SODIUM; 35 MG CHOLESTEROL; 2 G DIETARY FIBER.

REDUCED FAT AND SODIUM

57 Spaghetti Pie

Makes 8 servings

Spaghetti is the perfect crust for this pie, featuring pizza-like ingredients. Fresh oregano and basil are wonderful additions. To save time, shred mozzarella cheese in your food processor.

6 ounces spaghetti, cooked
  and drained
¼ cup egg substitute
1 tablespoon + 1 teaspoon reduced-
  calorie tub margarine
1 tablespoon grated Parmesan cheese
1 teaspoon parsley flakes
15 ounces lean ground beef, broiled
  2 minutes
2 teaspoons olive oil

1 cup diced green bell pepper
½ cup chopped scallions
½ cup tomato sauce
½ teaspoon dried basil
½ teaspoon crushed fennel seeds
¼ teaspoon salt
⅛ teaspoon freshly ground black
  pepper
2¼ ounces shredded part-skim
  mozzarella cheese

1. In large bowl, toss together spaghetti, egg substitute, margarine, Parmesan cheese and parsley flakes; set aside.

2. In large nonstick skillet, heat oil; add beef, bell pepper and scallions. Cook, stirring to break up meat, 4-5 minutes, until vegetables are tender and beef is no longer pink. Stir in remaining ingredients except mozzarella cheese; simmer 5-6 minutes, until sauce thickens. Remove from heat and stir in 1 ounce of the mozzarella cheese.

3. Preheat oven to 350°F. Spray a 10" pie plate with nonstick cooking spray; spread spaghetti in plate, lining bottom and pressing up sides to form a crust. Spoon beef mixture into crust. Cover with foil and bake 30 minutes. Uncover and sprinkle with the remaining mozzarella cheese; bake 15 minutes longer. Let stand 10 minutes before serving.

EACH SERVING PROVIDES: 1/2 FAT; 2 PROTEINS; 1/2 VEGETABLE; 1 BREAD; 5 OPTIONAL CALORIES.
PER SERVING: 276 CALORIES, 15 G PROTEIN; 15 G FAT; 18 G CARBOHYDRATE; 274 MG SODIUM;
45 MG CHOLESTEROL; 1 G DIETARY FIBER.

REDUCED SODIUM AND CHOLESTEROL

58 Lamb Pinwheels with Lemon Sauce

Makes 4 servings

Currants, pignolias, cinnamon and mint are all important parts of the lamb filling.

FILLING:
1 tablespoon olive oil
1 cup diced unpared eggplant
½ cup chopped scallions
¾ pound lean ground lamb
2 tablespoons finely chopped fresh flat-leaf parsley
2 tablespoons chopped fresh mint
2 tablespoons currants
1 tablespoon + 1 teaspoon pignolias (pine nuts)
¼ teaspoon salt
¼ teaspoon cinnamon
⅛ teaspoon freshly ground black pepper
4 ounces curly lasagna noodles, cooked and drained (4 noodles)

SAUCE:
1 tablespoon + 1 teaspoon reduced-calorie tub margarine
1 tablespoon all-purpose flour
1 cup hot low-sodium chicken broth
¼ cup egg substitute
2 tablespoons fresh lemon juice

1. Preheat oven to 350°F. Line a 9" square baking pan with foil; set a small rack in pan and spray rack with nonstick cooking spray.

2. In large skillet, heat oil; add eggplant and scallions. Cook over medium-high heat, stirring frequently, 2 minutes. Stir in 2 tablespoons water; reduce heat to low and simmer, covered, until eggplant is soft, 2-3 minutes; cool slightly.

3. Add remaining filling ingredients except lasagna noodles to cooled eggplant mixture; mix until thoroughly combined. Spread mixture evenly over each lasagna strip. With sharp knife, cut each strip in half lengthwise. Roll up 1 strip jelly-roll style. Overlap second lasagna strip where first one ends, making sure curly end is facing the same way. Secure end with wooden pick. Repeat with remaining strips to make three more pinwheels. Place, curly end up, on rack in baking pan; cover with foil. Bake 40 minutes, until lamb is cooked through.

4. To prepare sauce, in small saucepan, melt margarine; whisk in flour. Cook, stirring constantly, 1 minute. Remove from heat. Gradually stir in hot broth until mixture is smooth. Return to heat and continue cooking, stirring constantly, until mixture thickens. In small bowl, beat egg substitute and lemon juice. Very slowly drizzle in hot broth, whisking constantly; return mixture to saucepan, whisking constantly to prevent curdling, until heated through. Do not boil. To serve, remove wooden picks from pinwheels; spoon lemon sauce evenly over top.

EACH SERVING PROVIDES: 1½ FATS; 2½ PROTEINS; ¾ VEGETABLE; 1¼ BREADS; 30 OPTIONAL CALORIES.
PER SERVING: 338 CALORIES; 24 G PROTEIN; 14 G FAT; 30 G CARBOHYDRATE; 271 MG SODIUM;
56 MG CHOLESTEROL; 2 G DIETARY FIBER.

REDUCED SODIUM

59 Mostaccioli with Spiced Veal Sauce

Makes 4 servings

Mostaccioli—little mustaches—are similiar in shape to penne, but shorter. Richly spiced with cinnamon and cloves, this dish is wonderful for a wintry night.

1 tablespoon + 1 teaspoon extra virgin olive oil
2 tablespoons finely chopped onion
2 garlic cloves, finely chopped
5 ounces lean ground veal
½ teaspoon paprika
Pinch ground cinnamon
Pinch ground cloves

1 bay leaf
½ cup dry white wine
1 cup canned Italian tomatoes, crushed
Salt and freshly ground black pepper to taste
6 ounces mostaccioli rigati (ridged pasta), cooked and drained
2 tablespoons grated Romano cheese

1. Preheat oven to 425°F. Spray an 8" square baking pan with nonstick cooking spray.

2. In medium saucepan, heat oil; add onion and garlic. Sauté, stirring, until onion is translucent, 2 minutes.

3. Add veal; sauté until meat loses its pink color. Stir in paprika, cinnamon, cloves, bay leaf, wine, tomatoes, salt and pepper to taste; simmer 15 minutes. Stir in pasta and 1 tablespoon of the Romano cheese.

4. Transfer mixture to prepared pan; remove bay leaf. Sprinkle with the remaining 1 tablespoon Romano cheese. Cover and bake 10 minutes.

EACH SERVING PROVIDES: 1 FAT; 1 PROTEIN; ½ VEGETABLE; 2 BREADS; 40 OPTIONAL CALORIES.
PER SERVING: 298 CALORIES; 14 G PROTEIN; 9 G FAT; 36 G CARBOHYDRATE; 162 MG SODIUM;
32 MG CHOLESTEROL; 2 G DIETARY FIBER.

REDUCED FAT AND SODIUM

Stuffed Pasta

Few things have a way of bringing family and friends together than sitting down to share a hearty one-dish meal, such as lasagna. The colors peeking through almost translucent ravioli, cannelloni, tortellini and manicotti also have magical properties, hinting at the promise of surprise fillings or the combination of tastes when sauce and pasta become one. Stuffed pasta dishes can require some extra time, but the additional preparation is a labor of love well worth the final result. These recipes also offer endless possibilities. Discover your favorite fillings—the subtle taste of Stuffed Shells with Walnut Sauce, savory meat fillings like Curried Turkey Manicotti or Mexican Stuffed Shells, or the classic herbed flavor of Pesto Stuffed Shells. Wonton wrappers are a wonderful, easy way to fill pasta, and Wonton Ravioli and Turkey Ravioli are just two tasty examples. Lasagna lovers are well rewarded—colorful Green and White Lasagna, Sausage and Pepper Lasagna and Ratatouille Lasagna are some unique variations on this stuffed and layered classic. Herbed Manicotti with Tomato-Olive Salsa, Spinach-Goat Cheese Stuffed Shells and Artichoke-Stuffed Manicotti showcase popular ingredients that are popping up in restaurants everywhere. These filled and layered dishes are the stuff dreams are made of.

61 Hearts of Palm-Zucchini Shells

Makes 2 servings

An impressive first course that's loaded with delicately flavored vegetables. We've chosen to serve these chilled stuffed shells on a bed of greens with a drizzle of vinaigrette. Use spinach pasta shells for a colorful variation.

½ cup drained coarsely chopped
  canned hearts of palm
½ cup coarsely shredded zucchini
1 tablespoon chopped fresh flat-leaf
  parsley
1 tablespoon + 1 teaspoon olive oil
2 teaspoons lemon juice

¼ teaspoon salt
⅛ teaspoon freshly ground black
  pepper
1½ ounces jumbo pasta shells,
  cooked and drained (about 6)
2 cups mixed salad greens

1. In medium bowl, combine hearts of palm, zucchini and parsley.

2. To prepare vinaigrette, in small bowl, whisk together olive oil, lemon juice, salt and pepper. Add 1 tablespoon vinaigrette to vegetables; mix lightly with fork to moisten. Stuff pasta shells evenly with vegetable mixture. Cover and refrigerate until well chilled. Refrigerate remaining vinaigrette.

3. To serve, divide salad greens between two serving plates. Top each with 3 stuffed shells; drizzle with remaining vinaigrette.

EACH SERVING (3 SHELLS) PROVIDES: 2 FATS; 3 VEGETABLES; 1 BREAD.
PER SERVING: 181 CALORIES; 4 G PROTEIN; 10 G FAT; 21 G CARBOHYDRATE; 281 MG SODIUM;
0 MG CHOLESTEROL; 2 G DIETARY FIBER.

CHOLESTEROL-FREE

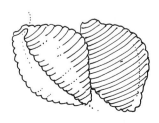

Vegetable-Stuffed Shells

Makes 2 servings

Monterey Jack cheese and basil jazz up the veggies in this recipe, which is great served as a side dish with grilled chicken breasts.

2 teaspoons reduced-calorie tub margarine
½ cup thinly sliced leeks (white part only)
½ cup coarsely shredded carrot
½ cup coarsely shredded yellow squash

½ cup coarsely shredded zucchini
¼ teaspoon dried basil
1½ ounces jumbo pasta shells, cooked and drained (about 6)
1 ounce coarsely shredded reduced-fat Monterey Jack cheese

1. Preheat oven to 350°F. Spray an 8" square baking pan with nonstick cooking spray.

2. In large nonstick skillet, melt margarine; add leeks. Cook over medium-high heat, stirring frequently, until soft, about 5 minutes. Add carrots, yellow squash and zucchini; stir to combine. Cook until vegetables are soft, about 3 minutes. Stir in basil.

3. Fill shells evenly with vegetable mixture; sprinkle evenly with cheese. Place in prepared pan; cover with foil. Bake 15 minutes, until heated through.

EACH SERVING PROVIDES: ½ FAT; ½ PROTEIN; 2 VEGETABLES; 1 BREAD.
PER SERVING: 178 CALORIES; 8 G PROTEIN; 6 G FAT; 25 G CARBOHYDRATE; 145 MG SODIUM; 10 MG CHOLESTEROL; 2 G DIETARY FIBER.

REDUCED SODIUM AND CHOLESTEROL

63 **Stuffed Shells with Walnut Sauce**

Makes 4 servings

A creamy walnut sauce coats shells stuffed with pumpkin puree and Parmesan cheese. Try this as a fun first course for Thanksgiving.

SAUCE:
1 ounce walnuts
½ cup part-skim ricotta cheese
½ cup chicken broth
1 tablespoon chopped fresh parsley
1 teaspoon grated lemon peel
Salt to taste

FILLING:
1½ cups canned pumpkin puree
¾ ounce grated Parmesan cheese
¼ teaspoon ground nutmeg
Salt and freshly ground black
   pepper to taste
6 ounces jumbo pasta shells,
   cooked and drained (about 24)

1. To prepare sauce, in food processor, chop walnuts. Add remaining sauce ingredients; puree until smooth.

2. To prepare filling, in small bowl, combine pumpkin, Parmesan cheese, nutmeg, salt and pepper.

3. Preheat oven to 350°F. Fill each shell with 1 level tablespoon filling; place in 13x9" baking pan. Spoon sauce over shells; cover with foil; bake 20 minutes.

EACH SERVING PROVIDES: 1 PROTEIN; 3/4 VEGETABLE; 2 BREADS; 5 OPTIONAL CALORIES.
PER SERVING: 306 CALORIES; 14 G PROTEIN; 10 G FAT; 43 G CARBOHYDRATE; 269 MG SODIUM;
14 MG CHOLESTEROL; 3 G DIETARY FIBER.

REDUCED FAT AND CHOLESTEROL

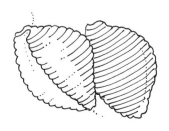

Mexican Stuffed Shells

Makes 4 servings

Pasta shells hold all the taco-like ingredients in this dish, which you can eat with your hands or a knife and fork.

13 ounces lean ground beef, broiled 2 minutes
½ cup chopped onion
1 garlic clove, minced
1 teaspoon chili powder
¼ teaspoon ground cumin
¼ teaspoon dried oregano
¼ teaspoon salt

½ cup spicy or mild salsa
¼ cup light sour cream
3 ounces jumbo pasta shells, cooked and drained (about 12)
1½ ounces coarsely shredded reduced-fat sharp cheddar cheese
½ cup shredded lettuce
2 tablespoons diced seeded tomato

1. Preheat oven to 350°F. Spray an 11x7" baking pan with nonstick cooking spray.

2. In large nonstick skillet, combine beef, onion and garlic. Cook over medium-high heat, stirring frequently to break up beef, until beef is browned and onion is translucent, about 5 minutes.

3. Add chili powder, cumin, oregano and salt; toss to mix well. Cook 1 minute. Stir in salsa; cook, stirring frequently, 5 minutes. Remove from heat; stir in sour cream. Let cool slightly.

4. Stuff shells evenly with meat mixture, mounding slightly. Arrange shells in baking pan; cover with foil. Bake 15 minutes; uncover and sprinkle evenly with cheese. Bake, uncovered, just until cheese melts, 1-2 minutes. Top shells evenly with lettuce and tomato.

EACH SERVING (3 SHELLS) PROVIDES: 3 PROTEINS; 3/4 VEGETABLE; 1 BREAD; 25 OPTIONAL CALORIES.
PER SERVING: 406 CALORIES; 24 G PROTEIN; 24 G FAT; 22 G CARBOHYDRATE; 463 MG SODIUM;
82 MG CHOLESTEROL; 1 G DIETARY FIBER.

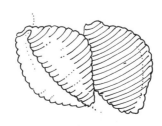

STUFFED PASTA
Slim Ways with Pasta

65 Spinach and Goat Cheese-Stuffed Shells

Makes 4 servings

Frozen spinach and canned tomatoes may make this dish a zip to prepare, but flavorful herbs and tart goat cheese make it tasty.

2 cups drained thawed frozen chopped spinach (one 10-ounce package)
1 cup part-skim ricotta cheese
3 ounces goat cheese, crumbled
3 ounces jumbo pasta shells (about 12), cooked and drained

2 teaspoons olive or vegetable oil
1 small garlic clove, minced
¼ teaspoon dried rosemary
¼ teaspoon dried sage
¼ teaspoon dried thyme
2 cups drained canned tomatoes, diced (reserve 2 tablespoons juice)

1. Preheat oven to 350°F. Spray an 11x7" baking pan with nonstick cooking spray.

2. In medium bowl, combine spinach, ricotta, goat cheese and 1 tablespoon water. Spoon mixture evenly into shells; arrange in baking pan.

3. To prepare sauce, in medium saucepan, heat oil; add garlic, rosemary, sage and thyme. Cook over medium-high heat, stirring constantly, 1 minute. Stir in tomatoes and the reserved 2 tablespoons juice; cook just until heated through. Spoon sauce evenly over stuffed shells. Bake 10 minutes, until heated through.

EACH SERVING PROVIDES: ½ FAT; 2 PROTEINS; 2 VEGETABLES; 1 BREAD.
PER SERVING: 300 CALORIES; 17 G PROTEIN; 14 G FAT; 29 G CARBOHYDRATE; 563 MG SODIUM; 19 MG CHOLESTEROL; 4 G DIETARY FIBER.

REDUCED CHOLESTEROL

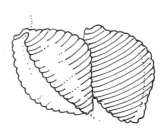

Pesto-Stuffed Shells

Makes 4 servings

The heady aroma of basil is more than enough reason to make these creamy shells. They're a great first course for a summer meal.

1 cup thinly sliced mushrooms
¼ teaspoon dried thyme
1 cup diced red bell pepper
½ cup diced yellow summer squash
10 ounces drained cooked chick-peas
½ cup sliced scallions
1 garlic clove
1 cup packed fresh basil leaves

1 cup part-skim ricotta cheese
1 ounce toasted pine nuts or walnuts
1½ ounces grated Parmesan cheese
¼ teaspoon freshly ground black pepper
3 ounces jumbo pasta shells, cooked and drained (about 12)

1. Heat large nonstick skillet over medium-high heat; add mushrooms and thyme. Cook 6 minutes, stirring occasionally. Add bell pepper and squash; cook 5 minutes, or until tender-crisp. Remove from heat; stir in chick-peas and scallions.

2. To prepare pesto, in food processor, process garlic until finely chopped; add basil and ricotta. Reserve 1 tablespoon pine nuts and 1 tablespoon Parmesan; add remaining pine nuts, Parmesan cheese and ground pepper; process until smooth.

3. Stir pesto into vegetable mixture; spoon evenly into cooked shells. Garnish with reserved Parmesan cheese and pine nuts. Serve at room temperature.

EACH SERVING PROVIDES: ½ FAT; 3 PROTEINS; 1½ VEGETABLES; 1 BREAD.
PER SERVING: 395 CALORIES; 24 G PROTEIN; 14 G FAT; 46 G CARBOHYDRATE; 286 MG SODIUM;
27 MG CHOLESTEROL; 4 G DIETARY FIBER.

REDUCED SODIUM AND CHOLESTEROL

STUFFED PASTA
Slim Ways with Pasta

67 Turkey Ravioli

Makes 4 servings

Ground turkey is a great substitute for beef in meat-based sauces and stuffings. Look for vegetable-flavored wonton skins to create a festive party dish.

14 ounces ground turkey
3/4 ounce shredded part-skim
  mozzarella cheese
2 tablespoons chopped fresh basil
1/4 teaspoon salt
1/8 teaspoon ground white pepper
20 wonton skins (3" squares)

1/2 cup evaporated skimmed milk
2 teaspoons all-purpose flour
1/4 teaspoon chopped shallot
2 teaspoons grated Parmesan cheese
1/4 teaspoon ground nutmeg
Chopped parsley to garnish

1. In large nonstick skillet, bring 6 cups water to a boil. In medium bowl, combine turkey, mozzarella, basil, salt and pepper.

2. Arrange wonton skins on work surface. Place 1 tablespoon turkey mixture in center of each wonton skin; with a pastry brush dipped in water, moisten edges. Fold one corner diagonally over filling to make a triangle. Press edges firmly together with fork or pastry crimper. Cover ravioli with damp towel until all are done.

3. Reduce heat under water to a simmer; add ravioli and cook 4-6 minutes, until tender and turkey is cooked, turning once. Remove with slotted spoon to bowl.

4. To prepare sauce, in small saucepan, over medium heat, combine evaporated milk, flour and shallot. Whisk until sauce thickens slightly and coats the back of a spoon; stir in Parmesan cheese and nutmeg. Spoon sauce over ravioli. Garnish with chopped parsley.

EACH SERVING (5 RAVIOLI) PROVIDES: 1/4 MILK; 3 PROTEINS; 1 BREAD; 10 OPTIONAL CALORIES.
PER SERVING: 277 CALORIES; 26 G PROTEIN; 9 G FAT; 23 G CARBOHYDRATE; 314 MG SODIUM;
77 MG CHOLESTEROL; 0 G DIETARY FIBER.

REDUCED FAT AND SODIUM

68 **Wonton Ravioli**

Makes 4 servings

In a delightful departure from the usual tomato, this light and colorful sauce of basil and red bell pepper brightens ravioli, stuffed with ricotta, spinach and an echo of red pepper.

SAUCE:
2 teaspoons olive oil
2 medium red bell peppers, thinly
   sliced
½ cup diced carrot
1 medium onion, thinly sliced
   and separated into rings
1½ cups drained crushed tomatoes
1 small Bartlett pear, pared, cored
   and diced

2 tablespoons chopped fresh basil
1 teaspoon crushed fennel seeds

RAVIOLI:
½ cup thawed frozen chopped
   spinach, squeezed dry
½ cup part-skim ricotta cheese
¼ cup diced roasted red bell pepper
2 tablespoons chopped fresh basil
20 wonton skins (3" squares)

1. To prepare sauce, in medium saucepan, heat olive oil; add peppers, carrot and onion. Cook, stirring frequently, over medium heat 6-7 minutes, until vegetables are very soft.

2. Add remaining sauce ingredients; bring to a boil. Cover; reduce heat to low and simmer 40 minutes, stirring occasionally.

3. To prepare filling, in medium bowl, combine spinach, ricotta, roasted pepper and basil.

4. Arrange wonton skins on work surface. Place 1 tablespoon spinach mixture in center of each wonton skin; with pastry brush dipped in water, moisten edges. Fold one corner diagonally over filling to make a triangle. Press edges firmly together with fork or pastry crimper. Cover ravioli with damp towel until all are filled.

5. To cook ravioli, in large nonstick skillet, bring 6 cups water to a boil. Reduce heat under water to a simmer; add ravioli and cook 5-6 minutes, gently turning over once. Remove with slotted spatula to large serving bowl. Spoon sauce over ravioli.

EACH SERVING (5 RAVIOLI AND ½ CUP SAUCE) PROVIDES: ½ FAT; ½ PROTEIN; 2½ VEGETABLES; 1 BREAD; ¼ FRUIT.
PER SERVING: 229 CALORIES; 10 G PROTEIN; 6 G FAT; 37 G CARBOHYDRATE; 224 MG SODIUM; 10 MG CHOLESTEROL; 4 G DIETARY FIBER.

REDUCED FAT AND CHOLESTEROL

69 Kreplach (Noodle Turnovers)

Makes 6 servings

A savory filling of ground chicken, parsley and onion fill these miniature turnovers, which are cooked pasta-style. Serve in chicken soup or as a side dish on its own.

1 cup + 2 tablespoons all-purpose flour
1 egg
Pinch salt
2 teaspoons reduced-calorie tub
   margarine

2 tablespoons minced onion
8 ounces cooked chicken, ground
1 teaspoon chopped fresh parsley
¼ teaspoon salt
Freshly ground black pepper to taste

1. To prepare dough, spoon 1 cup of the flour into a mound on work surface. Make a well in the center and add the egg, 1¹/₂ teaspoons water and the salt. With fork, beat egg lightly to combine; gradually work in flour to form a dough. Knead about 10 minutes, until smooth and elastic. Gather dough into a ball; wrap in plastic wrap or wax paper; set aside 30 minutes.

2. To prepare filling, in small nonstick skillet, melt margarine; add onion. Cook, stirring, until onion is translucent, 5 minutes. Transfer to medium bowl; stir in chicken, parsley, salt and pepper.

3. Sprinkle clean work surface with the remaining 2 tablespoons flour. Roll out dough to ¹/₈" thickness; cut into twelve 3" squares, rerolling scraps as needed.

4. Place a scant tablespoon of filling in center of each square; fold one corner diagonally over filling to make a triangle. Press edges firmly together with fork or pastry crimper. Set aside 20 minutes.

5. In large pot of boiling water, cook kreplach, covered, 20 minutes, or until they float to the surface. Remove with slotted spoon to large serving bowl.

EACH SERVING (2 KREPLACH) PROVIDES: 1¹/₂ PROTEINS; 1 BREAD; 10 OPTIONAL CALORIES.
PER SERVING: 176 CALORIES; 14 G PROTEIN; 5 G FAT; 18 G CARBOHYDRATE; 168 MG SODIUM;
69 MG CHOLESTEROL; 1 G DIETARY FIBER.

REDUCED SODIUM

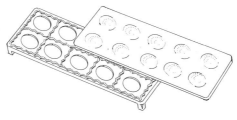

STUFFED PASTA
Slim Ways with Pasta

Cannelloni "Knishes"

Makes 4 servings

If you like knishes, you'll love this pasta variation. It's a fun finger food for parties, served with spicy brown mustard for dipping.

15 ounces all-purpose potatoes,
   pared and cut into 1" cubes
2 teaspoons vegetable oil
½ cup finely chopped onion
¼ teaspoon salt

⅛ teaspoon freshly ground black
   pepper
4 ounces small cannelloni pasta
   shells, cooked and drained
   (16 shells)

1. In medium saucepan, cook potatoes in boiling water to cover until tender, about 15 minutes; drain. Return to saucepan and mash with fork until smooth.

2. In small nonstick skillet, heat oil; add onion. Cook, stirring frequently, just until onion is translucent, 2 minutes. Add to potatoes with salt and pepper; combine with fork.

3. Preheat oven to 350°F. Spray shallow baking dish with nonstick cooking spray.

4. Working with 1 cannelloni shell at a time, stand shell on end and, with fingers, firmly press in about 1½ tablespoons potato filling. Arrange "knishes" in pan; cover with foil. Bake until hot, about 20 minutes.

EACH SERVING (4 KNISHES) PROVIDES: ½ FAT; ¼ VEGETABLE; 2 BREADS; 5 OPTIONAL CALORIES.
PER SERVING: 191 CALORIES; 5 G PROTEIN; 3 G FAT; 36 G CARBOHYDRATE; 142 MG SODIUM;
0 MG CHOLESTEROL; 2 G DIETARY FIBER.

REDUCED FAT AND SODIUM; CHOLESTEROL-FREE

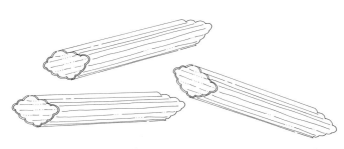

STUFFED PASTA
Slim Ways with Pasta

Artichoke-Stuffed Manicotti

Makes 4 servings

Manicotti is baked with a creamy ricotta-artichoke filling and then topped with melted mozzarella.

2 teaspoons olive oil
¾ cup chopped red onion
2 cups thawed frozen artichoke hearts, coarsely chopped
1 cup sliced mushrooms
2 tablespoons chopped fresh flat-leaf parsley
2 teaspoons chopped fresh thyme
¼ teaspoon salt

½ cup chicken broth
½ cup part-skim ricotta cheese
2 teaspoons grated Parmesan cheese
½ cup tomato sauce
3 ounces manicotti shells, cooked and drained (about 6 shells)
1½ ounces shredded part-skim mozzarella cheese

1. To prepare filling, in large nonstick skillet, heat olive oil; add onion. Sauté 2-3 minutes, until tender. Add artichoke hearts, mushrooms, 1 tablespoon of the parsley, the thyme and salt; sauté 2 minutes.

2. Preheat oven to 350°F. Add chicken broth to skillet; cook, stirring frequently, 6-7 minutes, until liquid evaporates. Remove skillet from heat; stir in ricotta and Parmesan cheese.

3. Spread sauce in bottom of an 8" square baking pan. Spoon artichoke filling evenly into the manicotti shells; place over sauce in pan. Cover with foil; bake 20 minutes. Remove foil. Sprinkle mozzarella cheese and the remaining parsley over top of manicotti; bake 10-12 minutes, or until cheese melts and filling is hot.

EACH SERVING PROVIDES: ½ FAT; 1 PROTEIN; 2 VEGETABLES; 1 BREAD; 20 OPTIONAL CALORIES.
PER SERVING: 235 CALORIES; 13 G PROTEIN; 8 G FAT; 30 G CARBOHYDRATE; 593 MG SODIUM;
16 MG CHOLESTEROL; 5 G DIETARY FIBER.

REDUCED CHOLESTEROL

STUFFED PASTA
Slim Ways with Pasta

Herbed Manicotti with Tomato-Olive Salsa

Makes 6 servings

Creamy manicotti with pepper jack cheese is served with a salsa of fresh plum tomatoes and Calamata olives. This dish is wonderful as an appetizer or paired with salad for a light lunch.

1 1/4 cups part-skim ricotta cheese
1 1/2 ounces shredded pepper jack cheese
2 tablespoons egg substitute
2 tablespoons chopped fresh parsley
2 tablespoons chopped fresh basil
4 1/2 ounces manicotti shells, cooked and drained (about 6)

BECHAMEL SAUCE:
3 tablespoons reduced-calorie tub margarine
3 tablespoons all-purpose flour
1 1/2 cups low-fat (1%) milk
1/4 teaspoon salt
1/4 teaspoon ground red pepper

SALSA:
3/4 cup chopped seeded plum tomatoes
9 large Calamata olives, pitted and sliced

1. In small bowl, combine ricotta, pepper jack cheese, egg substitute and 1 1/2 teaspoons each of the parsley and basil. Fill manicotti shells evenly with mixture; set aside. Preheat oven to 350°F.

2. To prepare sauce, in medium saucepan, melt margarine. Whisk in flour; cook over low heat, stirring constantly, 1 minute. Remove from heat. Gradually whisk in milk, salt and pepper until mixture is smooth. Place over medium-high heat and cook, stirring constantly, until sauce thickens and bubbles, 1 minute.

3. Spread 1/4 cup of the sauce in an 11 x 7" baking pan; arrange manicotti in pan. Pour remaining sauce over top. Bake 30 minutes, then place under broiler to lightly brown top, 2 minutes.

4. Meanwhile, prepare salsa: In small bowl, combine tomatoes, olives and the remaining parsley and basil. To serve, spoon salsa over manicotti.

EACH SERVING PROVIDES: 1/4 MILK; 1 FAT; 1 PROTEIN; 1/4 VEGETABLE; 1 BREAD; 30 OPTIONAL CALORIES.
PER SERVING: 274 CALORIES; 14 G PROTEIN; 13 G FAT; 27 G CARBOHYDRATE; 531 MG SODIUM;
26 MG CHOLESTEROL; 1 G DIETARY FIBER.

Curried Turkey Manicotti

73

Makes 3 servings

Raisins and curry make up the sweet and spicy sauce that covers these savory turkey and spinach-filled shells. Serve a cooling yogurt, chopped cucumber and mint sauce on the side.

SAUCE:
½ cup finely chopped onion
½ cup finely chopped green bell
  pepper
¼ cup finely chopped celery
1 tablespoon canola or vegetable oil
2 tablespoons all-purpose flour
1 tablespoon curry powder
¾ teaspoon ground cumin
2 cups low-sodium chicken broth
2 cups seeded chopped plum
  tomatoes
2 tablespoons dark raisins

FILLING:
7 ounces ground turkey or chicken
½ cup finely shredded zucchini
½ cup finely shredded fresh spinach
1 egg
½ teaspoon salt
⅛ teaspoon freshly ground black
  pepper
4½ ounces manicotti shells, cooked
  and drained (about 6)

1. Reserve 1 tablespoon each onion, bell pepper and celery; set aside for filling. To prepare sauce, in large nonstick skillet, heat oil; add remaining onion, bell pepper and celery. Cook over medium-high heat, stirring frequently, until onion is translucent, about 3 minutes.

2. Add flour, curry and cumin to vegetables; toss lightly to coat. Cook 1 minute. Stir in chicken broth; bring to a boil. Reduce heat to medium; cook, stirring, until mixture thickens slightly. Add tomatoes and raisins; stir to combine. Reduce heat to low; simmer, covered, stirring frequently, 10 minutes.

3. Preheat oven to 350°F. Spray an 11x7" baking pan with nonstick cooking spray.

4. In medium bowl, combine reserved vegetables and all filling ingredients, mixing thoroughly. Spoon about 3 tablespoons filling into each manicotti shell. Arrange filled shells in pan; top with sauce. Cover with foil; bake 25 minutes, or until filling is set and sauce is bubbly.

EACH SERVING PROVIDES: 1 FAT; 2 PROTEINS; 3 VEGETABLES; 2 BREADS; 65 OPTIONAL CALORIES.
PER SERVING: 434 CALORIES; 24 G PROTEIN; 15 G FAT; 53 G CARBOHYDRATE; 518 MG SODIUM;
119 MG CHOLESTEROL; 5 G DIETARY FIBER.

REDUCED FAT

74 Ratatouille Lasagna

Makes 6 servings

A basic ratatouille becomes a veggie-rich layer in this lasagna, featuring a creamy ricotta filling and white sauce.

2 tablespoons olive or canola oil
1 cup halved sliced zucchini
1 cup diced green bell pepper
1 cup sliced mushrooms
1 cup diced unpared eggplant
¾ cup sliced onion
2 garlic cloves, minced
1¼ cups chopped seeded plum
  tomatoes
2 tablespoons chopped fresh basil
2 tablespoons chopped fresh parsley

¾ teaspoon salt
¼ teaspoon freshly ground black
  pepper
1 cup part-skim ricotta cheese
¾ ounce grated Parmesan cheese
1 egg
6 ounces whole-wheat lasagna
  noodles, cooked and drained
  (6 noodles)
Bechamel Sauce (recipe follows)

1. To prepare ratatouille, in large nonstick skillet, heat oil; add zucchini, bell pepper, mushrooms, eggplant, onion and garlic. Cook over medium-high heat, stirring, until eggplant softens and vegetables are crisp-tender, 5 minutes. Stir in tomatoes, basil, parsley, salt, black pepper and ¼ cup water; bring to a boil. Reduce heat to low; simmer, stirring frequently, 10 minutes. Let cool.

2. Preheat oven to 350°F. Spray an 11x7" baking pan with nonstick cooking spray.

3. To prepare filling, in medium bowl, combine ricotta, Parmesan cheese and egg, blending well. Place 3 lasagna noodles in prepared baking pan; layer with half the cheese mixture, the ratatouille and the remaining cheese mixture; cover with the remaining 3 lasagna noodles. Pour prepared Bechamel Sauce over top. Cover with foil; bake 30 minutes, or until bubbly. Let stand 10 minutes before serving.

EACH SERVING PROVIDES: 1¹/₂ FATS; 1 PROTEIN; 2 VEGETABLES; 1 BREAD; 50 OPTIONAL CALORIES.
PER SERVING: 299 CALORIES; 14 G PROTEIN; 13 G FAT; 35 G CARBOHYDRATE; 490 MG SODIUM;
53 MG CHOLESTEROL; 5 G DIETARY FIBER.

BECHAMEL SAUCE:

In medium saucepan, melt 2 tablespoons reduced-calorie tub margarine. Whisk in 2 tablespoons all-purpose flour and cook over low heat, stirring constantly, 1 minute. Remove from heat. Gradually whisk in 1 cup low-fat (1%) milk and pinch salt and nutmeg until mixture is smooth. Return to heat; increase heat to medium-high and cook, stirring constantly, until mixture thickens and bubbles, 1 minute.

Green and White Lasagna

Makes 12 servings

Use a glass baking pan to show off the colorful layers in this dish, just right for a crowd. Serve with a salad of cucumber and tomato chunks, dressed with oil, vinegar and fresh herbs.

2 tablespoons reduced-calorie tub margarine
1½ tablespoons all-purpose flour
1½ cups evaporated skimmed milk
¼ teaspoon freshly ground black pepper
Pinch ground nutmeg
9 ounces shredded Fontina cheese (reserve 2 tablespoons)
2 cups drained thawed frozen chopped spinach (one 10-ounce package)

2 cups drained thawed frozen chopped broccoli (one 10-ounce package)
12 ounces rinsed drained cooked cannellini beans
½ cup chopped roasted red pepper (reserve 2 tablespoons)
9 ounces curly or plain lasagna noodles, cooked and drained (9 noodles)

1. To prepare cheese sauce, in medium saucepan, melt margarine; stir in flour. Cook, stirring constantly, 2 minutes. Whisk in milk, black pepper and nutmeg; cook, stirring constantly, until mixture comes to a boil and thickens slightly. Remove from heat and stir in cheese; continue stirring until cheese melts and mixture is smooth.

2. Preheat oven to 350°F. In medium bowl, combine spinach, broccoli, cannellini beans and red pepper. Spray a 13x9" baking pan with nonstick cooking spray.

3. Arrange one-third of the lasagna noodles in prepared pan; spread with one-third of the vegetable mixture; top with one-third of the cheese sauce. Repeat layering twice, ending with cheese sauce. Sprinkle reserved cheese and red pepper on top. Cover with foil and bake 30 minutes; remove foil and bake 10 minutes longer. Let stand 10 minutes before serving.

EACH SERVING PROVIDES: ¼ MILK; ¼ FAT; 1½ PROTEINS; ¾ VEGETABLE; 1 BREAD; 5 OPTIONAL CALORIES.
PER SERVING: 246 CALORIES; 15 G PROTEIN; 8 G FAT; 28 G CARBOHYDRATE; 315 MG SODIUM;
26 MG CHOLESTEROL; 3 G DIETARY FIBER.

REDUCED FAT

STUFFED PASTA
Slim Ways with Pasta

Sausage and Pepper Lasagna

Makes 4 servings

This dish combines two Italian favorites for those of us who can't get enough of a good thing.

2 teaspoons olive oil
6 ounces Italian turkey sausage, casings removed
½ cup chopped red or yellow bell pepper
½ cup chopped green bell pepper
½ cup chopped onion
1 teaspoon dried oregano
¼ teaspoon fennel seeds, crushed
2 cups canned no-salt-added tomatoes, crushed

1 cup part-skim ricotta cheese
1 ½ ounces shredded part-skim mozzarella cheese
1 egg
¾ ounce grated Parmesan cheese
⅛ teaspoon dried red pepper flakes
4 ounces curly or plain lasagna noodles, cooked and drained (4 noodles)

1. To prepare sauce, in large saucepan, heat oil; add turkey sausage, bell pepper, onion, ¹/2 teaspoon of the oregano and the fennel seeds. Cook, stirring, over medium-high heat, until turkey is browned and vegetables are tender, about 7 minutes. Add tomatoes and bring to a boil. Reduce heat to low; simmer, stirring occasionally, until thickened, 20-25 minutes.

2. Preheat oven to 350°F.

3. In medium bowl, combine ricotta, mozzarella, egg, Parmesan cheese, the remaining ¹/2 teaspoon oregano and the red pepper flakes.

4. Arrange lasagna noodles on work surface; spread equal amounts of ricotta mixture over each noodle. Roll up from long end, jelly-roll style. Spread ¹/2 cup of the sauce in an 8" square baking pan; arrange rolls over sauce. Spoon remaining sauce over top. Cover with foil; bake 30 minutes, until bubbly. Let stand 10 minutes before serving.

EACH SERVING PROVIDES: ¹/2 FAT; 3 PROTEINS; 1³/4 VEGETABLES; 1¹/4 BREADS; 5 OPTIONAL CALORIES.
PER SERVING: 390 CALORIES; 26 G PROTEIN; 17 G FAT; 34 G CARBOHYDRATE; 556 MG SODIUM;
113 MG CHOLESTEROL; 2 G DIETARY FIBER.

STUFFED PASTA
Slim Ways with Pasta

Sauced Pasta

There is nothing quite like arriving home and being welcomed by the smell of pasta sauce cooking—except perhaps being asked to taste a spoonful! The most memorable dishes pair pasta and sauce perfectly. Matching shapes and textures to the flavors of a sauce can become almost instinctive, but there are some basic rules of thumb. Delicate sauces lend themselves to thinner pasta, while robust meat sauces work well with hearty tubular macaroni and spiral shapes. Roasted peppers, capers, olives, sun-dried tomatoes, walnuts or pignolias are ingredients used to create a variety of sauces as well as the basics—onions, garlic, canned tomatoes, herbs and spices. Pasta and Pizza is wonderful served together or as appetizer and main dish. Grilled Turkey Sausage with Pasta and Penne with Grilled Vegetables may start a new trend in outdoor grilling, edging out typical barbecue fare. Fresh herbs provide flavor and fragrance in Tri-Color Pasta with Herbed Butter, Fettuccine with Herbed Prosciutto and Herbed Rotelle with Balsamic Vinegar. To impress dinner guests, serve Pasta with Salmon in Vodka Cream, Minted Shrimp with Orzo or Fusilli with Walnut Cream Sauce. Vegetables make a colorful statement in Cavatelli with Radicchio, Arugula and Bacon and Fettuccine with Goat Cheese and Peppers. With all these dishes, the secret is in the sauce!

78 Tri-Color Pasta with Herbed "Butter"

Makes 4 servings

This easy, inexpensive dish features a fragrant no-cook sauce. Serve with sole fillets or a salad of fresh mozzarella balls and dried tomatoes for a special meal.

6 ounces tri-color rotini, cooked and drained

2 tablespoons + 2 teaspoons reduced-calorie tub margarine

1 tablespoon chopped fresh basil, sage or oregano

¼ teaspoon garlic salt

Freshly ground black pepper to taste

Place pasta, margarine, herbs, garlic salt and pepper in large serving bowl; toss until margarine is melted.

EACH SERVING PROVIDES: 1 FAT; 2 BREADS.

PER SERVING: 190 CALORIES; 6 G PROTEIN; 4 G FAT; 32 G CARBOHYDRATE; 205 MG SODIUM;

0 MG CHOLESTEROL; 2 G DIETARY FIBER.

REDUCED FAT; CHOLESTEROL-FREE

79 Rotelle with Olive-Caper Sauce

Makes 4 servings

This piquant sauce of capers, olives and dried tomatoes is easy to fix and works well with radiatore or small shells. Serve with freshly grated Parmesan cheese.

10 dried tomato halves
2 teaspoons olive oil
½ cup chopped red onion
20 small Calamata olives, pitted and chopped
¼ cup coarsely chopped basil
1 tablespoon dried marjoram

⅛ teaspoon freshly ground black pepper
½ cup low-sodium chicken broth
2 tablespoons (1 ounce) dry white wine
1 tablespoon drained rinsed capers
3 ounces rotelle, cooked and drained

1. In medium bowl, soak tomatoes in boiling water to cover 2 minutes; drain. Chop tomatoes.

2. In large nonstick skillet, heat oil; add onion, olives, tomatoes, basil, marjoram and pepper. Cook, stirring frequently, 2-3 minutes, until onion is tender. Stir in broth, wine and capers; reduce heat to low and simmer 10-12 minutes, until liquid reduces slightly.

3. Place pasta in large serving bowl; pour sauce over pasta. Toss to mix well.

EACH SERVING PROVIDES: 1 FAT; 1½ VEGETABLES; 1 BREAD; 10 OPTIONAL CALORIES.
PER SERVING: 188 CALORIES; 5 G PROTEIN; 8 G FAT; 25 G CARBOHYDRATE; 541 MG SODIUM;
0 MG CHOLESTEROL; 2 G DIETARY FIBER.

CHOLESTEROL-FREE

80 **Pasta Puttanesca**

Makes 4 servings

Legend has it that Italian "ladies of the night" created this dish to further satisfy their clients' appetites! Our version uses tuna; other popular variations include anchovies and capers.

¼ cup golden raisins
1 tablespoon olive oil
½ cup chopped onion
2 garlic cloves, minced
1 ½ cups chopped drained canned low-sodium tomatoes
1 cup low-sodium tomato sauce

6 pitted large ripe olives, sliced
¼ teaspoon ground red pepper
8 ounces drained canned water-packed tuna
Freshly ground black pepper to taste
6 ounces spaghetti, cooked and drained

1. In small bowl, soak raisins in ⅓ cup warm water.

2. In large nonstick skillet, heat oil; add onion and garlic. Cook 7-10 minutes, until soft.

3. Add raisins and their soaking liquid, tomatoes, tomato sauce, olives and red pepper. Increase heat to high; cook 3-5 minutes, until slightly thickened.

4. Break tuna into chunks; stir into tomato mixture. Cook just until heated through. Season to taste with black pepper. Transfer to large serving bowl.

5. Add spaghetti; toss to coat well.

EACH SERVING PROVIDES: 1 FAT; 1 PROTEIN; 1½ VEGETABLES; 2 BREADS; ½ FRUIT.
PER SERVING: 346 CALORIES, 24 G PROTEIN; 6 G FAT; 50 G CARBOHYDRATE; 293 MG SODIUM; 24 MG CHOLESTEROL; 4 G DIETARY FIBER.

REDUCED FAT AND CHOLESTEROL

81 Fusilli with Walnut Cream Sauce

Makes 4 servings

This velvety sauce is a match for the long spiral strands of fusilli and slivers of dried tomatoes. To quickly toast walnuts, place in microwave on High 1-2 minutes or until they release their aroma.

1 cup part-skim ricotta cheese
½ cup evaporated skimmed milk
2 ounces toasted walnuts
¼ cup fresh parsley
1 garlic clove

⅛ teaspoon salt
2 cups thawed frozen broccoli florets
  (one 10-ounce package)
8 dried tomato halves, cut into strips
3 ounces short or long fusilli

1. To prepare sauce, in food processor, combine ricotta cheese, milk, walnuts, parsley, garlic and salt; process until smooth.

2. Transfer sauce to large nonstick skillet; add broccoli and dried tomatoes. Cook over low heat 5-8 minutes, until tomatoes are softened and sauce is heated through. Add fusilli to skillet; toss to coat with sauce.

EACH SERVING PROVIDES: ¼ MILK; 1 FAT; 1½ PROTEINS; 2 VEGETABLES; 1 BREAD.
PER SERVING: 318 CALORIES; 17 G PROTEIN; 14 G FAT; 33 G CARBOHYDRATE; 210 MG SODIUM;
20 MG CHOLESTEROL; 2 G DIETARY FIBER.

REDUCED CHOLESTEROL

82 Herbed Rotelle with Balsamic Vinegar

Makes 4 servings

Balsamic vinegar is essential to this dish. Its fruitiness gives the pasta a unique taste.

4 dried tomato halves
2 teaspoons olive oil
2 cups cubed zucchini
2 garlic cloves, minced
2 cups canned plum tomatoes
1 teaspoon chopped fresh rosemary,
 or 1 teaspoon dried

1 tablespoon chopped fresh oregano,
 or 1 teaspoon dried
1 tablespoon balsamic vinegar
6 ounces rotelle pasta (spirals), cooked
 and drained
1 tablespoon + 1 teaspoon grated
 Parmesan cheese

1. In small bowl, soak dried tomatoes in boiling water to cover 2 minutes; drain and chop.

2. In large nonstick skillet, heat oil; add zucchini and garlic. Cook, stirring frequently, 4-5 minutes. Stir in dried and plum tomatoes, rosemary and oregano; simmer 15-20 minutes, until sauce thickens, stirring to break up tomatoes. Stir in vinegar.

3. Place pasta in large serving bowl; pour sauce over pasta and toss to mix well. Sprinkle with Parmesan cheese; toss and serve.

EACH SERVING PROVIDES: 1/2 FAT; 2 1/2 VEGETABLES; 2 BREADS; 10 OPTIONAL CALORIES.
PER SERVING: 231 CALORIES; 9 G PROTEIN; 4 G FAT; 42 G CARBOHYDRATE; 235 MG SODIUM;
1 MG CHOLESTEROL; 3 G DIETARY FIBER.

REDUCED FAT AND CHOLESTEROL

SAUCED PASTA
Slim Ways with Pasta

83 Tri-Color Noodles with Broccoli

Makes 4 servings

Garlic, wine, anchovies, olives—staples of an Italian pantry—are featured in this richly flavored dish. It's great with crusty Italian bread.

1 ½ cups fresh broccoli florets
3 ounces tri-colored ruffled noodles
1 tablespoon olive oil
½ cup chopped onion
1 ounce drained anchovy fillets,
  coarsely chopped
2 garlic cloves, minced

¼ cup dry white wine
¼ cup chopped fresh flat-leaf parsley
6 pitted large black olives, sliced
2 teaspoons chopped fresh thyme
¼ teaspoon salt

1. In large pot of boiling water, cook broccoli 2 minutes. With slotted spoon, remove to serving bowl; reserve liquid in pot.

2. Return liquid in pot to a boil. Add noodles; cook 7-9 minutes, or until tender; drain and reserve.

3. Meanwhile, in large nonstick skillet, heat oil; add onion, anchovies and garlic. Cook, stirring constantly, 4 minutes, or until garlic is tender.

4. Add broccoli, wine, parsley, olives, thyme and salt to skillet; cook, stirring, 3-4 minutes, or until liquid evaporates.

5. Add broccoli mixture to noodles; toss to mix well.

EACH SERVING PROVIDES: 1 FAT; 1 VEGETABLE; 1 BREAD; 35 OPTIONAL CALORIES.
PER SERVING: 170 CALORIES; 7 G PROTEIN; 6 G FAT; 21 G CARBOHYDRATE; 476 MG SODIUM;
24 MG CHOLESTEROL; 1 G DIETARY FIBER.

REDUCED CHOLESTEROL

SAUCED PASTA
Slim Ways with Pasta

84 Pasta Primavera

Makes 4 servings

A great basic recipe you can recreate again and again with your favorite vegetables.

¼ cup low-sodium chicken broth
1 tablespoon + 1 teaspoon olive oil
1½ cups broccoli florets
1 medium red bell pepper, thinly sliced
1 cup halved mushrooms
1 cup frozen peas
½ cup sliced scallions

2 garlic cloves, minced
1 ounce (2 tablespoons) dry white wine
4½ ounces fettuccine, cooked and drained
1 tablespoon + 1 teaspoon grated Parmesan cheese

1. In large nonstick skillet, heat broth and 2 teaspoons of the oil; add broccoli, pepper, mushrooms, peas, scallions and garlic. Cook, stirring frequently, 4-5 minutes, until vegetables are tender. Stir in wine; cook 1 minute longer.

2. Place fettuccine in serving bowl; toss with the remaining 2 teaspoons oil. Add vegetable mixture; toss to mix well. Sprinkle with Parmesan cheese.

EACH SERVING PROVIDES: 1 FAT; 2 VEGETABLES; 2 BREADS; 20 OPTIONAL CALORIES.

PER SERVING: 235 CALORIES, 10 G PROTEIN; 7 G FAT; 34 G CARBOHYDRATE; 97 MG SODIUM; 32 MG CHOLESTEROL; 3 G DIETARY FIBER.

REDUCED FAT AND SODIUM

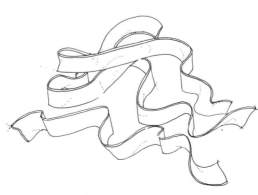

SAUCED PASTA
Slim Ways with Pasta

85 Rotelle with Vegetable Chili

Makes 4 servings

Try this chili with pasta and you may never go back to rice! Jalapeño pepper is hot-hot-hot—so adjust to your taste.

1 tablespoon + 1 teaspoon extra virgin olive oil
½ cup chopped onion
2 garlic cloves, chopped
¼ cup coarsely chopped carrot
¼ cup coarsely chopped celery
2 teaspoons chili powder
½ teaspoon ground cumin
¼ teaspoon dried oregano
Pinch ground cloves
Pinch ground allspice
Pinch ground coriander

1 teaspoon finely chopped seeded jalepeño pepper
1 cup cubed red and/or yellow bell pepper
2 cups canned Italian tomatoes, chopped
8 ounces drained cooked pinto beans
4½ ounces rotelle pasta, cooked and drained
¼ cup light sour cream
¼ cup chopped scallions
1 tablespoon chopped fresh cilantro

1. In large saucepan, heat oil; add onion, garlic, carrot and celery. Sauté, stirring occasionally, until onion is translucent, 2 minutes.

2. Add chili powder, cumin, oregano, cloves, allspice, coriander and jalapeño pepper; sauté, stirring, 2 minutes. Add ¼ cup water; simmer 5 minutes.

3. Add bell pepper; cook 5 minutes, stirring occasionally. Stir in tomatoes. Simmer, stirring occasionally, 35 minutes.

4. Add beans and heat through. Place pasta in large serving bowl; pour chili on top and toss to coat. Ladle evenly into four shallow bowls; top each serving with 1 tablespoon sour cream; sprinkle evenly with scallions and cilantro.

EACH SERVING PROVIDES; 1 FAT; 1 PROTEIN; 2 VEGETABLES; 1½ BREADS; 25 OPTIONAL CALORIES.
PER SERVING: 313 CALORIES; 12 G PROTEIN; 8 G FAT; 51 G CARBOHYDRATE; 224 MG SODIUM;
5 MG CHOLESTEROL; 6 G DIETARY FIBER.

REDUCED FAT AND CHOLESTEROL

SAUCED PASTA
Slim Ways with Pasta

Radiatore with Roasted Beets, Fennel and Onions

Makes 4 servings

While the oven is on, plan to roast some beef or poultry and potatoes on the next rack and cook two meals at once.

2 cups diced pared beets
1½ cups diced fennel
1½ cups diced onions
2 teaspoons canola oil
½ teaspoon fennel seeds
Salt and freshly ground black pepper to taste
6 ounces radiatore, cooked and drained

2 teaspoons extra virgin olive or walnut oil
2 tablespoons grated Parmesan cheese
1 tablespoon chopped fresh flat-leaf parsley

1. Preheat oven to 350°F. Spray an 11x7" baking pan with nonstick cooking spray.

2. Combine beets, fennel, onions, canola oil, fennel seeds, salt and pepper to taste in prepared pan; toss until well mixed. Roast, stirring occasionally, 45 minutes, until vegetables are just tender.

3. Stir pasta into vegetable mixture; add olive oil, Parmesan cheese and parsley; toss to combine.

EACH SERVING PROVIDES: 1 FAT; 2½ VEGETABLES; 2 BREADS; 20 OPTIONAL CALORIES.
PER SERVING: 270 CALORIES; 9 G PROTEIN; 6 G FAT; 45 G CARBOHYDRATE; 141 MG SODIUM;
2 MG CHOLESTEROL; 3 G DIETARY FIBER.

REDUCED FAT, SODIUM AND CHOLESTEROL

87 Linguine with Winter Greens

Makes 4 servings

The pungent tastes of Swiss chard and broccoli rabe go well together. You can make this dish with spinach if Swiss chard is out of season.

2 cups coarsely chopped trimmed
    broccoli rabe, thick ends removed
6 ounces linguine
1 tablespoon + 1 teaspoon olive oil
1 cup chopped onion
⅛ teaspoon ground red pepper
½ cup low-sodium chicken broth

2 cups coarsely chopped red or green
    Swiss chard
1 tablespoon fresh lemon juice
¼ teaspoon garlic powder
1 tablespoon + 1 teaspoon grated
    provolone cheese

1. In large pot of boiling water, cook broccoli rabe 2 minutes. With slotted spoon, remove to bowl; reserve liquid in pot.

2. Return liquid in pot to a boil; add pasta and cook 7-8 minutes, until tender; drain and return to pot.

3. Meanwhile, in large nonstick skillet, heat oil. Add onion and ground red pepper; cook, stirring frequently, 3-4 minutes, until onion is tender. Add broth; cook 4-5 minutes, or until most of the liquid evaporates.

4. Add broccoli rabe, Swiss chard, lemon juice and garlic powder to skillet; cook 2 minutes, until chard has wilted. Add vegetable mixture to linguine in pot; toss well. Place in serving bowl and sprinkle with provolone cheese.

EACH SERVING PROVIDES: 1 FAT; 2½ VEGETABLES; 2 BREADS; 15 OPTIONAL CALORIES.
PER SERVING: 239 CALORIES; 8 G PROTEIN; 6 G FAT; 38 G CARBOHYDRATE; 87 MG SODIUM; 2 MG CHOLESTEROL; 3 G DIETARY FIBER.

REDUCED FAT, SODIUM AND CHOLESTEROL

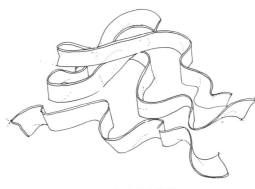

SAUCED PASTA
Slim Ways with Pasta

88 **Pasta with Spicy Eggplant**

Makes 4 servings

Eggplant is a basic ingredient in many delicious Italian dishes. This sauce goes well with a variety of pasta shapes and tastes best at room temperature.

4 cups cubed unpared eggplant
1 tablespoon + 1 teaspoon olive oil
1 tablespoon red wine vinegar
2 tablespoons chopped scallion
1 garlic clove, minced
¼ teaspoon dried red pepper flakes

¼ teaspoon salt
6 ounces spaghetti, cooked and drained
2 cups canned plum tomatoes, chopped
2 tablespoons chopped fresh parsley

1. Steam eggplant in vegetable steamer over simmering water 10 minutes, or until soft. Place in large serving bowl.

2. In small bowl, whisk together oil, vinegar, scallion, garlic, red pepper flakes and salt.

3. Pour oil mixture over warm eggplant. Stir in spaghetti, tomatoes and parsley. Toss to mix well. Serve at room temperature.

EACH SERVING PROVIDES: 1 FAT; 3 VEGETABLES; 2 BREADS.
PER SERVING: 246 CALORIES; 8 G PROTEIN; 6 G FAT; 43 G CARBOHYDRATE; 338 MG SODIUM;
0 MG CHOLESTEROL; 3 G DIETARY FIBER.

REDUCED FAT; CHOLESTEROL-FREE

89 Rigatoni with Sautéed Peppers and Basil

Makes 4 servings

Serve this peppery pasta with a salad of garden tomatoes and red onion. An especially sturdy dish, it can be chilled to travel to a picnic or your office.

1 tablespoon + 1 teaspoon extra virgin olive oil
2 garlic cloves, finely chopped
⅛ teaspoon dried red pepper flakes (or to taste)
½ teaspoon fennel seeds, lightly crushed
3 large red and yellow bell peppers, cut into ½" strips

6 ounces rigatoni, cooked and drained (reserve 2 tablespoons cooking water)
2 tablespoons grated Parmesan cheese
1 tablespoon chopped fresh basil
1 tablespoon chopped fresh flat-leaf parsley

1. In large nonstick skillet, combine oil, garlic, pepper flakes and fennel seeds. Cook over medium heat 3 minutes, stirring frequently and being careful not to burn garlic.

2. Add peppers; increase heat slightly and sauté, stirring occasionally, until peppers are tender (not limp), 3-4 minutes. Transfer to large serving bowl.

3. Add pasta, cheese, basil and parsley to bowl; toss to mix well. If mixture seems dry, add reserved pasta cooking water.

EACH SERVING PROVIDES: 1 FAT; 3 VEGETABLES; 2 BREADS; 15 OPTIONAL CALORIES.
PER SERVING: 246 CALORIES; 8 G PROTEIN; 6 G FAT; 41 G CARBOHYDRATE; 53 MG SODIUM;
2 MG CHOLESTEROL; 3 G DIETARY FIBER.

REDUCED FAT, SODIUM AND CHOLESTEROL

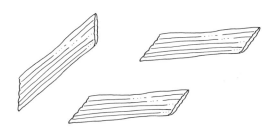

SAUCED PASTA
Slim Ways with Pasta

90 Penne with Grilled Vegetables

Makes 4 servings

This dish merits a visit to a roadside farm stand to choose freshly harvested vegetables and herbs. Choose the roasting option if you need time to prepare other dishes and can't tend to the grill.

1 large red bell pepper, halved
1 large yellow bell pepper, halved
1 small eggplant, unpared, cut lengthwise into ¼" slices
1 medium onion, thickly sliced
1 medium zucchini, cut lengthwise into ¼" slices
4 medium mushrooms, stems removed
1 tablespoon + 1 teaspoon extra virgin olive oil
2 garlic cloves, finely chopped

1 teaspoon chopped fresh rosemary
1 teaspoon chopped fresh thyme
1 teaspoon chopped fresh sage
6 ounces penne, cooked and drained (reserve 2 tablespoons cooking water)
2 tablespoons grated Parmesan cheese
1 tablespoon chopped fresh flat-leaf parsley

1. Preheat broiler. Line broiler pan with foil. Place peppers in pan, cut-sides down; broil until blackened all over, 15-20 minutes. Place in glass or metal bowl and cover tightly; let cool to room temperature, then skin, seed and cut into bite-size pieces.

2. Meanwhile, prepare outdoor grill following manufacturer's directions. Grill eggplant, onion, zucchini and mushrooms, turning frequently, until browned and tender. Cut into pieces and add to peppers.

3. In medium nonstick skillet, heat oil; add garlic, rosemary, thyme and sage. Sauté 2 minutes, stirring. Add vegetables, pasta, Parmesan cheese and parsley; toss to mix well. If mixture seems too dry, add reserved pasta cooking water.

*Alternately: Vegetables can be diced, tossed with 2 teaspoons of the oil, salt and pepper to taste and roasted in a 400°F oven in a shallow pan until tender. Proceed as above; reduce sauté oil to 2 teaspoons.

EACH SERVING PROVIDES: 1 FAT; 4 VEGETABLES; 2 BREADS; 15 OPTIONAL CALORIES.
PER SERVING: 274 CALORIES; 9 G PROTEIN; 6 G FAT; 47 G CARBOHYDRATE; 58 MG SODIUM;
2 MG CHOLESTEROL; 4 G DIETARY FIBER.

REDUCED FAT, SODIUM AND CHOLESTEROL

91 # Cavatelli with Radicchio, Arugula and Bacon

Makes 4 servings

Have all your prep work for this recipe done before you begin cooking, since ingredients will be added to the sauté quickly to prevent overcooking.

2 teaspoons extra virgin olive oil
2 garlic cloves, finely chopped
2 teaspoons chopped fresh rosemary
1 small head radicchio, torn into bite-size pieces
½ cup arugula leaves
1 slice crisp cooked bacon, drained and crumbled

6 ounces cavatelli, cooked and drained (reserve 2 tablespoons cooking water)
1 tablespoon balsamic vinegar
1 tablespoon grated Parmesan cheese
Salt and freshly ground black pepper to taste

1. In large nonstick skillet, heat oil; add garlic and rosemary. Sauté 2 minutes. Add radicchio; increase heat to medium-high and cook, tossing, one minute. Add arugula and bacon; continue to toss, 30 seconds. Add pasta and vinegar; toss until liquid evaporates.

2. Transfer to large serving bowl; add Parmesan cheese, salt and pepper to taste; toss to mix well. If mixture seems too dry, add reserved pasta cooking water.

EACH SERVING PROVIDES: ½ FAT; ½ VEGETABLE; 2 BREADS; 20 OPTIONAL CALORIES.
PER SERVING: 201 CALORIES; 7 G PROTEIN; 4 G FAT; 34 G CARBOHYDRATE; 56 MG SODIUM;
2 MG CHOLESTEROL; 1 G DIETARY FIBER.

REDUCED FAT, SODIUM AND CHOLESTEROL

92 Fettuccine with Herbed Prosciutto

Makes 4 servings

Super simple and simply delicious! Be careful not to overcook the asparagus in this dish the first time around, as it gets heated again with the fettuccine.

1 tablespoon + 1 teaspoon margarine
4 garlic cloves, minced
2 tablespoons chopped fresh sage, or 2 teaspoons dried
2 tablespoons chopped fresh thyme, or 2 teaspoons dried
½ cup low-sodium chicken broth

2 ounces thinly sliced prosciutto, coarsely chopped
6 blanched asparagus spears, cut into 1" pieces
3 ounces fettuccine, cooked and drained

1. In large nonstick skillet, melt margarine; add garlic, sage and thyme. Cook, stirring constantly, 2 minutes. Stir in broth, prosciutto and asparagus; simmer 1-2 minutes, until heated through.

2. Add fettuccine to skillet; toss to mix well. Cook 1 minute longer to blend flavors.

EACH SERVING PROVIDES: 1 FAT; ½ PROTEIN; ¼ VEGETABLE; 1 BREAD; 5 OPTIONAL CALORIES.
PER SERVING: 156 CALORIES; 7 G PROTEIN; 6 G FAT; 18 G CARBOHYDRATE; 270 MG SODIUM;
29 MG CHOLESTEROL; 1 G DIETARY FIBER.

Fettuccine with Prosciutto and Vegetables

93

Makes 4 servings

Here's a hearty yet flavorful recipe that works equally well as a side dish. Try using frozen vegetables if you need to toss it together quickly.

1 tablespoon + 1 teaspoon reduced-calorie tub margarine	½ cup peas
2 ounces prosciutto, cut into thin strips	½ cup low-sodium chicken broth
½ cup sliced scallions	3 ounces fettuccine, cooked and drained
2 garlic cloves, minced	½ medium tomato, cut into wedges
1 cup sliced carrots	2 teaspoons grated Parmesan cheese
1 cup sliced zucchini	Freshly ground black pepper to taste

1. In medium skillet, over medium-high heat, melt margarine; add prosciutto, scallions and garlic. Cook 3 minutes, stirring frequently. Add carrots, zucchini, peas and broth; bring to a boil. Lower heat to medium; simmer 5 minutes.

2. Place fettuccine in large serving bowl. Spoon vegetable mixture over fettuccine; add tomato, Parmesan cheese and pepper to taste; toss to mix well.

EACH SERVING PROVIDES: 1/2 FAT; 1/2 PROTEIN; 1 1/2 VEGETABLES; 1 1/4 BREADS; 10 OPTIONAL CALORIES.
PER SERVING: 153 CALORIES; 9 G PROTEIN; 4 G FAT; 21 G CARBOHYDRATE; 399 MG SODIUM;
34 MG CHOLESTEROL; 2 G DIETARY FIBER.

REDUCED FAT

SAUCED PASTA
Slim Ways with Pasta

94 Pasta with Arugula and Ham

Makes 4 servings

A variation on carbonara sauce, ham is cooked in wine and added to a creamy blend of ricotta and Parmesan.

1 tablespoon + 1 teaspoon olive oil
2 garlic cloves, minced
6 ounces cubed cooked lean ham
¼ cup dry white wine

3 ounces fusilli, cooked and drained
4 cups arugula leaves
½ cup part-skim ricotta cheese
1 tablespoon grated Parmesan cheese

1. In large nonstick skillet, heat oil; add garlic. Cook, stirring constantly, 1-2 minutes, until tender. Stir in ham and wine; cook 2-3 minutes, or until most of the liquid evaporates.

2. Add pasta, arugula, ricotta and Parmesan cheese to skillet; cook, stirring to coat pasta, 1-2 minutes, or until heated through.

EACH SERVING PROVIDES: 1 FAT; 2 PROTEINS; 2 VEGETABLES; 1 BREAD; 20 OPTIONAL CALORIES.
PER SERVING: 244 CALORIES; 17 G PROTEIN; 10 G FAT; 19 G CARBOHYDRATE; 590 MG SODIUM;
33 MG CHOLESTEROL; 1 G DIETARY FIBER.

REDUCED CHOLESTEROL

95 Spaghetti with Onion-Anchovy Sauce

Makes 4 servings

With just a few ingredients and three simple steps, this dish is easy, economical and one you'll grow to rely on when you want a tasty meal in a pinch.

1 teaspoon olive oil
1 teaspoon canola oil
3 cups thinly sliced red onions
4 anchovy fillets, well drained and patted dry
6 ounces spaghetti, cooked and drained (reserve 2 tablespoons cooking water)

2 tablespoons grated Parmesan cheese
1 tablespoon chopped fresh flat-leaf parsley
Freshly ground black pepper to taste

1. In medium saucepan, combine oil, onions and 2 tablespoons water. Cover and cook over very low heat, stirring occasionally, 1 hour, until onions are very soft.

2. With wooden spoon, mash anchovies into onions; cook 30 seconds. Stir in pasta, Parmesan cheese, parsley and reserved pasta cooking water. Transfer to large serving bowl; season with pepper to taste.

EACH SERVING PROVIDES: 1/2 FAT; 1 1/2 VEGETABLES; 2 BREADS; 20 OPTIONAL CALORIES.
PER SERVING: 247 CALORIES; 10 G PROTEIN; 4 G FAT; 43 G CARBOHYDRATE; 209 MG SODIUM;
4 MG CHOLESTEROL; 1 G DIETARY FIBER.

REDUCED FAT AND CHOLESTEROL

Who says you can't have your pasta and pizza, too? Cheesy tomato pita wedges are a zesty accompaniment to the creamy pepper sauce on linguine.

2 small tomatoes
1 small pita (1 ounce), split
1 teaspoon olive oil
1½ ounces provolone cheese, shredded
¾ ounce grated Parmesan cheese
2 tablespoons slivered fresh basil
½ cup julienned red bell pepper

½ cup julienned green bell pepper
½ teaspoon chopped garlic
¼ cup lowfat 1% milk
2¼ ounces linguine, cooked and drained
1 ounce smoked turkey breast, slivered

1. Seed and chop one tomato. Thinly slice remaining tomato; reserve for pizza.

2. To prepare pizza, preheat oven to 425°F. Drizzle pita halves evenly with oil; arrange the sliced tomato around edges. Sprinkle the provolone cheese, ¼ ounce of the Parmesan cheese and 1 tablespoon of the basil over tomatoes.

3. Bake 6-8 minutes, or until bubbly and golden around the edges. Cut into wedges.

4. While pizza is baking, prepare pasta sauce: Spray medium nonstick skillet with nonstick cooking spray; add peppers. Sauté over medium-low heat, 3-4 minutes. Add garlic and the chopped tomato; cook 3 minutes, or until soft and most of the liquid has evaporated. Stir in milk and the remaining ½ ounce of the Parmesan cheese.

5. Add pasta, the remaining 1 tablespoon basil and the turkey; toss to mix well. To serve, place half the pasta in center of 2 dishes. Surround each with half the pizza wedges; serve hot or warm.

EACH SERVING PROVIDES: 2 BREADS; 2 PROTEINS; 1/2 FAT; 1 1/2 VEGETABLES; 10 OPTIONAL CALORIES.
PER SERVING: 368 CALORIES; 22 G PROTEIN; 13 G FAT; 52 G CARBOHYDRATE; 645 MG SODIUM;
30 MG CHOLESTEROL; 3 G DIETARY FIBER.

REDUCED FAT

Fettuccine with Goat Cheese and Peppers

97

Makes 4 servings

Robust tastes—goat cheese, dried tomatoes and Calamata olives—make this dish memorable. To set off the colorful peppers, use half spinach and half plain fettuccine.

8 dried tomato halves
1 tablespoon olive oil
1 cup sliced scallions
2 garlic cloves, minced
1 medium red bell pepper, thinly sliced
1 medium yellow bell pepper, thinly sliced
¼ cup chicken broth or dry vermouth
¼ cup slivered fresh basil

10 small Calamata olives, pitted and coarsely chopped
1 tablespoon rinsed drained capers
2 teaspoons dried oregano
6 ounces fettuccine, cooked and drained
4½ ounces herbed or plain goat cheese, crumbled

1. In medium bowl, soak tomatoes in boiling water to cover 2 minutes. Drain, reserving ¼ cup liquid. Thinly slice tomatoes; set aside.

2. In large nonstick skillet, heat oil; add scallions and garlic. Cook, stirring frequently, 2 minutes. Add peppers; cook, stirring, 3 minutes, until just tender. Stir in chicken broth; cook until liquid nearly evaporates.

3. Reduce heat to low; add tomatoes and reserved liquid, basil, olives, capers and oregano; simmer 5 minutes.

4. Place fettuccine in large serving bowl. Add goat cheese and toss until melted. Add pepper mixture; toss to mix well.

EACH SERVING PROVIDES: 1 FAT; 1½ PROTEINS; 2½ VEGETABLES; 2 BREADS; 3 OPTIONAL CALORIES.
PER SERVING: 354 CALORIES; 13 G PROTEIN; 16 G FAT; 42 G CARBOHYDRATE; 686 MG SODIUM;
40 MG CHOLESTEROL; 4 G DIETARY FIBER.

SAUCED PASTA
Slim Ways with Pasta

98 Angel Hair Pasta with Lemon and White Beans

Makes 4 servings

Delicate lemon sauce gilds angel hair in this refreshing, satisfying dish.

Zest of 1 lemon, finely grated
2 tablespoons fresh lemon juice
2 teaspoons margarine
2 teaspoons olive oil
¼ teaspoon freshly ground black
   pepper
½ cup low-sodium chicken broth

8 ounces drained cooked white beans
½ cup coarsely chopped basil
¼ cup chopped fresh parsley
4½ ounces angel hair pasta, cooked
   and drained
2 tablespoons grated Asiago cheese

1. In medium serving bowl, combine lemon zest, lemon juice, margarine, oil and pepper; set aside.

2. In large nonstick skillet, heat broth; add beans, basil and parsley. Cook, stirring frequently, 2-3 minutes, until heated through.

3. Add pasta and bean mixture to serving bowl; toss to mix well. Sprinkle with cheese.

EACH SERVING PROVIDES: 1 FAT; 1 PROTEIN; 1¹/₂ BREADS; 20 OPTIONAL CALORIES.
PER SERVING: 244 CALORIES; 10 G PROTEIN; 6 G FAT; 38 G CARBOHYDRATE; 272 MG SODIUM;
2 MG CHOLESTEROL; 3 G DIETARY FIBER.

REDUCED FAT AND CHOLESTEROL

99 Penne with Shrimp and Pepper Sauce

Makes 4 servings

This peppery sauce is a treat. Allow time to peel and devein the shrimp—you'll need the shells to make the shrimp stock.

12 medium unshelled shrimp
1 bay leaf
¼ teaspoon ground thyme
1 tablespoon + 1 teaspoon olive oil
2 cups cubed red bell peppers
1 cup low-sodium tomato sauce
½ cup chopped fresh parsley

¼ teaspoon salt
¼ teaspoon dried basil
Pinch dried red pepper flakes
¼ cup sliced scallions
3 ounces penne or other tubular
  pasta, cooked and drained

1. Peel and devein shrimp; set aside. Place shells in large nonstick skillet; add bay leaf, thyme and ³/₄ cup water. Bring to a boil; reduce heat and simmer 8 minutes, stirring, until shells turn opaque. Strain into small bowl, pressing shells to extract all liquid. Discard shells.

2. Wipe out skillet; heat oil. Add bell peppers and sauté 10-12 minutes, stirring, until peppers are soft; remove from heat and cool slightly. Place peppers in food processor with tomato sauce, parsley, salt, basil, red pepper flakes and reserved shrimp liquid; process until smooth.

3. Scrape stock puree into skillet. Add scallions and shrimp; cook 3 minutes, until shrimp turn pink, stirring occasionally. (If mixture becomes too thick, add water, 1 tablespoon at a time.) Place penne in large serving bowl; pour shrimp mixture over penne and toss to mix well.

EACH SERVING PROVIDES: 1 FAT; ¹/₂ PROTEIN; 1¹/₂ VEGETABLES; 1 BREAD.
PER SERVING: 208 CALORIES; 11 G PROTEIN; 6 G FAT; 29 G CARBOHYDRATE; 195 MG SODIUM;
43 MG CHOLESTEROL; 3 G DIETARY FIBER.

REDUCED FAT AND SODIUM

Minted Shrimp with Orzo

Makes 4 servings

The strong flavors of dried tomatoes and mint are a delightful contrast in this shrimp dish, cooked with white wine and served atop orzo.

1 tablespoon + 1 teaspoon olive oil	½ cup dry white wine
36 medium shrimp, shelled and deveined	½ cup low-sodium chicken broth
½ cup sliced scallions	2 tablespoons chopped fresh mint
6 dried tomato halves, soaked, drained and cut into strips	3 ounces orzo, cooked and drained

1. In large nonstick skillet, heat oil; add shrimp. Sauté just until pink, stirring constantly, 2 minutes. Remove to bowl; cover and keep warm.

2. To same skillet, add scallions and tomatoes; cook, stirring, until scallions are tender, 2-3 minutes.

3. Increase heat to high; stir, scraping all brown bits from bottom. Add wine and broth; lower heat and simmer 5 minutes, until liquid is reduced to about $^{1}/_{2}$ cup. Add shrimp and mint to skillet; cook, stirring, until heated through. To serve, divide orzo evenly among 4 plates; spoon shrimp and sauce evenly over top.

EACH SERVING PROVIDES: 1 FAT; 1$^{1}/_{2}$ PROTEINS; 1 VEGETABLE; 1 BREAD; 30 OPTIONAL CALORIES.
PER SERVING: 249 CALORIES; 21 G PROTEIN; 7 G FAT; 21 G CARBOHYDRATE; 143 MG SODIUM;
129 MG CHOLESTEROL; 2 G DIETARY FIBER.

REDUCED SODIUM

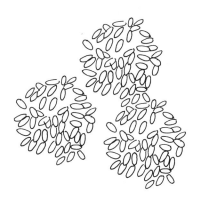

101 Pasta with Salmon in Vodka Cream

Makes 4 servings

Vodka sauce is the rage at many restaurants. This version with salmon is sure to satisfy. For a special meal, try it with black pasta—squid ink linguine—which is available at specialty food stores.

2 tablespoons + 2 teaspoons reduced-calorie tub margarine
1/4 cup finely chopped shallots
2 cups trimmed snow peas, halved diagonally
1/4 cup chicken broth

1/4 cup heavy cream
2 tablespoons vodka
6 ounces sliced smoked salmon, cut into strips
6 ounces spaghetti, cooked and drained

1. In large nonstick skillet, over medium-high heat, melt margarine; add shallots and sauté 3 minutes. Add snow peas; cook 3 minutes longer, stirring frequently.

2. Reduce heat to low; stir in chicken broth, cream and vodka. Cook until heated through; do not boil.

3. Place pasta in large serving bowl. Pour sauce over pasta; add salmon and toss to mix well.

EACH SERVING PROVIDES: 1 FAT; 1 1/2 PROTEINS; 1 VEGETABLE; 2 BREADS; 70 OPTIONAL CALORIES.
PER SERVING: 347 CALORIES; 16 G PROTEIN; 12 G FAT; 39 G CARBOHYDRATE; 481 MG SODIUM;
30 MG CHOLESTEROL; 3 G DIETARY FIBER.

102 Fettuccine with Tomato-Clam Sauce

Makes 4 servings

A new twist on red clam sauce—this one uses both dried tomatoes and tomato paste for intense flavor.

4 dried tomato halves
1 tablespoon + 1 teaspoon olive oil
½ cup chopped onion
1 ounce drained anchovy fillets,
  coarsely chopped
2 garlic cloves, minced
6 ounces drained canned whole clams

½ cup low-sodium chicken broth
½ cup clam and tomato juice blend
¼ cup tomato paste
½ teaspoon dried oregano
⅛ teaspoon dried red pepper flakes
3 ounces fettuccine, cooked
  and drained

1. In small bowl, soak tomatoes in boiling water to cover 2 minutes; drain. In mini food processor, puree tomatoes; set aside.

2. In large nonstick skillet, heat oil; add onion, anchovies and garlic. Cook, stirring frequently, 3-4 minutes, or until onion is tender. Add tomatoes and remaining ingredients except fettuccine. Bring to a boil; reduce heat to low and simmer 12-15 minutes.

3. Place fettuccine in serving bowl. Spoon clam sauce on top of fettuccine. Toss to mix well.

EACH SERVING PROVIDES: 1 FAT; 1 PROTEIN; 1¼ VEGETABLES; 1 BREAD; 5 OPTIONAL CALORIES.
PER SERVING: 238 CALORIES; 18 G PROTEIN; 7 G FAT; 25 G CARBOHYDRATE; 540 MG SODIUM;
53 MG CHOLESTEROL; 2 G DIETARY FIBER.

REDUCED FAT

SAUCED PASTA
Slim Ways with Pasta

103 Pasta with Smoked Mussels and Turkey

Makes 4 servings

An impressive company dish full of intense flavors.

4 cups slivered leeks, cut into 2" lengths

2 large vegetarian vegetable bouillon cubes

3 medium zucchini, halved lengthwise and cut into ¼" thick slices (3 cups)

1 tablespoon cornstarch

¼ cup white wine vinegar

2 tablespoons dry vermouth

1 tablespoon white wine Worcestershire sauce

2 cups sliced crimini or other fresh mushrooms

1 teaspoon chopped jalapeño pepper

6 ounces linguine, cooked and drained

5 ounces cubed cooked turkey

18 smoked mussels, drained

1. In medium nonstick skillet, bring leeks, bouillon cubes and 2 cups water to a boil; simmer 6 minutes. Increase heat to medium; add zucchini and cook, covered, 5 minutes, or until tender-crisp.

2. With slotted spoon, remove leeks and zucchini to large serving bowl; bring liquid in skillet to a boil. Cook 4 minutes, or until liquid is reduced to about ¾ cup.

3. In small cup, combine cornstarch and 2 tablespoons of the vinegar. Add to liquid in skillet and cook 1 minute, stirring constantly, until thickened. Remove from heat and stir in remaining vinegar, the vermouth and Worcestershire sauce. Pour over leek mixture.

4. Spray medium nonstick skillet with nonstick cooking spray; add mushrooms and jalapeño pepper. Sauté over high heat until golden brown, about 5-6 minutes. Add to leek mixture with linguine, turkey and mussels. Toss to mix well.

EACH SERVING PROVIDES: 2 PROTEINS; 4½ VEGETABLES; 2 BREADS; 40 OPTIONAL CALORIES.
PER SERVING: 355 CALORIES; 24 G PROTEIN; 4 G FAT; 57 G CARBOHYDRATE; 648 MG SODIUM;
39 MG CHOLESTEROL; 3 G DIETARY FIBER.

REDUCED FAT AND CHOLESTEROL

SAUCED PASTA
Slim Ways with Pasta

Ziti with Turkey Sauce

Makes 4 servings

A classic meat sauce without the meat—ground turkey stands in for beef beautifully in this zesty dish. You can substitute celery for fennel.

1 tablespoon + 1 teaspoon olive oil
½ cup chopped onion
½ cup diced fennel
½ cup diced carrot
12 ounces ground turkey
½ teaspoon dried oregano
¼ cup dry red wine

2 cups chopped canned tomatoes
1 cup low-sodium chicken broth
¼ cup low-sodium tomato paste
2 tablespoons chopped fresh parsley
6 ounces plain or ridged ziti, cooked and drained

1. In large Dutch oven, heat oil; add onion, fennel and carrot. Cook, stirring, 2-3 minutes.

2. Add turkey and oregano; cook 3-4 minutes, or until turkey is no longer pink, stirring to break up meat. Add wine; cook 2 minutes, or until liquid evaporates.

3. Stir in tomatoes, chicken broth, tomato paste and parsley; simmer 30 minutes, stirring occasionally.

4. Place ziti in large serving bowl. Spoon turkey sauce over ziti; toss to mix well.

EACH SERVING PROVIDES: 1 FAT; 2 PROTEINS; 2 VEGETABLES; 2 BREADS; 40 OPTIONAL CALORIES.
PER SERVING: 391 CALORIES; 23 G PROTEIN; 12 G FAT; 44 G CARBOHYDRATE; 323 MG SODIUM;
62 MG CHOLESTEROL; 4 G DIETARY FIBER.

REDUCED FAT AND SODIUM

105 Grilled Turkey Sausage with Pasta

Makes 4 servings

For an intriguing blend of sweet and spicy, sausage, zucchini and escarole are brushed with a molasses-mustard glaze, then grilled and tossed with pasta.

1½ tablespoons balsamic vinegar
1½ tablespoons grainy Dijon mustard
1 tablespoon light molasses
¼ cup low-sodium beef broth
1 tablespoon fresh lemon juice
2 teaspoons olive oil
¼ teaspoon salt
15 ounces sweet Italian turkey sausage

2 medium zucchini, quartered
 lengthwise
One 1-pound head escarole, trimmed
 and halved lengthwise
3 ounces radiatore,
 cooked and drained
12 cherry tomatoes, halved

1. To prepare mustard glaze, in small bowl, combine 1 tablespoon of the vinegar, 1 tablespoon of the mustard and 2 teaspoons of the molasses.

2. To prepare dressing, in large bowl, mix together remaining vinegar, mustard and molasses, the broth, lemon juice, oil and salt.

3. Place grill rack 5" from coals. Spray with nonstick cooking spray. Prepare grill according to manufacturer's directions. Brush sausage, zucchini and escarole evenly with mustard glaze.

4. Arrange sausage, zucchini and escarole on grill; cook 12 minutes, until sausage is cooked through, turning and brushing with glaze.

5. Cut sausage, zucchini and escarole into pieces. Add sausage, zucchini, escarole, pasta and tomatoes to dressing in bowl; toss to mix well.

EACH SERVING PROVIDES: ½ FAT; 3 PROTEINS; 5½ VEGETABLES; 1 BREAD; 20 OPTIONAL CALORIES.
PER SERVING: 314 CALORIES; 19 G PROTEIN; 14 G FAT; 30 G CARBOHYDRATE; 852 MG SODIUM;
91 MG CHOLESTEROL; 4 G DIETARY FIBER.

Radiatore with Grilled Sausage and Broccoli Rabe

Makes 4 servings

The pleasant, slightly bitter taste of broccoli rabe, also known as rapini, is the perfect complement to spicy turkey sausage.

10 ounces hot Italian turkey sausage
1 tablespoon + 1 teaspoon olive oil
1 cup chopped scallions
2 garlic cloves, minced
Pinch ground red pepper
2 cups broccoli rabe

1 cup low-sodium chicken broth
4½ ounces radiatore,
  cooked and drained
2 tablespoons grated provolone
  cheese
2 teaspoons low-sodium soy sauce

1. Preheat broiler. Broil sausage 5-7 minutes, turning once, until browned and cooked through; cut into thin diagonal slices.

2. Meanwhile, in large nonstick skillet, heat oil; add scallions, garlic and red pepper. Cook, stirring constantly, 2 minutes. Add broccoli rabe and ½ cup of the broth; cook 4-5 minutes, until tender.

3. Stir in radiatore, sausage, the remaining broth, the provolone cheese and soy sauce; cook until heated through and liquid is slightly reduced.

EACH SERVING PROVIDES: 1 FAT; 2 PROTEINS; 1½ VEGETABLES; 1½ BREADS; 25 OPTIONAL CALORIES.
PER SERVING: 301 CALORIES; 16 G PROTEIN; 13 G FAT; 30 G CARBOHYDRATE; 480 MG SODIUM;
62 MG CHOLESTEROL; 2 G DIETARY FIBER.

107 Chicken-Avocado Fettuccine

Makes 4 servings

A pasta dish alive with Mexican flavors—chicken, Monterey Jack cheese and avocado top fettuccine. Serve with salsa and a red onion-orange salad.

1 cup sliced mushrooms
2 teaspoons olive oil
8 ounces boneless skinless chicken breast, cut into ½" cubes
2 tablespoons chopped fresh flat-leaf parsley
1 tablespoon drained canned chopped green chilies

¼ teaspoon salt
½ cup evaporated skimmed milk
1½ ounces cubed Monterey Jack cheese
3 ounces fresh or dried spinach fettuccine, cooked and drained
2 ounces cubed avocado

1. Spray large nonstick skillet with nonstick cooking spray; add mushrooms. Cook over medium-high heat, stirring constantly, 2-3 minutes, until tender. Remove mushrooms to bowl.

2. To prepare sauce, in same skillet, heat oil. Add chicken, parsley, chilies and salt; cook, stirring constantly, 7-9 minutes, or until chicken is firm and no longer pink. Stir in milk, cheese and reserved mushrooms. Cook, stirring constantly, 5-6 minutes, or until sauce thickens and cheese melts.

3. Place fettuccine in large serving bowl; add avocado. Pour sauce over pasta; toss to mix well.

EACH SERVING PROVIDES: ¼ MILK; 1 FAT; 2 PROTEINS; ½ VEGETABLE; 1 BREAD.
PER SERVING: 237 CALORIES; 22 G PROTEIN; 9 G FAT; 17 G CARBOHYDRATE; 299 MG SODIUM;
68 MG CHOLESTEROL; 1 G DIETARY FIBER.

REDUCED SODIUM

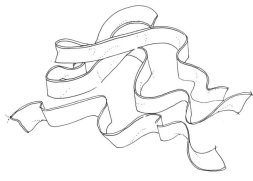

SAUCED PASTA
Slim Ways with Pasta

Vermicelli with Beef Sauce

Makes 4 servings

This meaty sauce combines beef and strips of ham in a savory tomato base.

14 ounces beef tenderloin or boneless
   shell steak, broiled 2 minutes
2 teaspoons unsalted margarine
2 teaspoons olive oil
¾ cup tomato paste
½ cup beef broth
½ cup chopped scallions
   (white part only)
1 bay leaf
1 whole clove

Pinch celery salt
Pinch ground nutmeg
Pinch thyme
Dash salt
1½ tablespoons flour, dissolved in ¼
   cup cold water
1 ounce cooked ham, cut into julienne
   strips
6 ounces vermicelli or spaghettini,
   cooked and drained

1. Mince beef finely with knife (do not grind).

2. In large heavy saucepan, heat margarine and oil; add beef. Cook over medium heat, stirring frequently, until meat loses its pink color, about 8 minutes. Add scallions and cook until softened, 5 minutes.

3. Add all remaining ingredients except flour mixture, ham and pasta. Bring to a boil; reduce heat and simmer 15 minutes.

4. Pour flour mixture into saucepan in a slow stream, stirring until thoroughly blended. Cook 15 minutes longer, until sauce is thickened. Add ham and cook until heated through.

5. Place pasta in large serving bowl; pour sauce over pasta and toss to combine.

EACH SERVING PROVIDES: 1 FAT; 3 PROTEINS; 1 VEGETABLE; 2 BREADS; 15 OPTIONAL CALORIES.
PER SERVING: 423 CALORIES; 30 G PROTEIN; 14 G FAT; 45 G CARBOHYDRATE; 690 MG SODIUM;
65 MG CHOLESTEROL; 4 G DIETARY FIBER.

109 Pasta Shells with Lamb Sauce

Makes 4 servings

Rosemary is perfectly suited to the strong flavors of lamb. If you can't find fresh, use 2 teaspoons dried, steeped in 1 tablespoon hot water for 2-3 minutes.

1 tablespoon + 1 teaspoon extra virgin olive oil
2 teaspoons finely chopped onion
1 garlic clove, finely chopped
2 tablespoons finely chopped fresh rosemary
4 ounces broiled lean ground lamb
3 juniper berries (optional)
1 cup canned Italian tomatoes, crushed

½ cup dry white wine
Salt and freshly ground black pepper to taste
6 ounces medium pasta shells, cooked and drained
1 tablespoon grated Pecorino Romano cheese

1. In medium saucepan, heat oil; add onion, garlic and rosemary. Sauté, stirring, until onion is translucent, 2 minutes.

2. Add lamb and juniper berries, if using. Increase heat to medium and sauté, stirring to break up lamb, 5 minutes. Add wine, tomatoes, 1/2 cup water and salt and pepper to taste. Bring to a boil; lower heat and simmer 30 minutes, stirring occasionally.

4. Add pasta; toss over low heat, 1-2 minutes. Transfer to large serving bowl. Add Romano cheese; toss to mix well.

EACH SERVING PROVIDES: 1 FAT; 1 PROTEIN; ½ VEGETABLE; 2 BREADS; 35 OPTIONAL CALORIES.
PER SERVING: 297 CALORIES; 14 G PROTEIN; 9 G FAT; 35 G CARBOHYDRATE; 141 MG SODIUM; 28 G CHOLESTEROL; 2 G DIETARY FIBER.

REDUCED FAT AND SODIUM

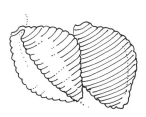

International Pasta

The variety of dishes from around the world in this chapter prove that pasta is a global staple—Italians alone haven't cornered the market on it! Some types of pasta used in these recipes can be found at Asian markets and specialty shops, as well as the gourmet sections of many supermarkets. Seafood, exotic spices and unique cheeses also distinguish these dishes. You will be rewarded for seeking out some of these less than run-of-the-mill ingredients when you taste the finished product. Tastes inspired by Spain, Greece, Thailand, Germany and Mexico are represented; we even feature our own interpretation of Chinese takeout favorites: Pork Lo Mein, Potstickers, Spicy Hunan Sesame Noodles and Thai-Style Noodles. Celebrate Mardi Gras with Pasta Jambalaya and Shrimp Creole Lasagna, or try Spaetzle with Paprika Sauce, creamy and rich. German Ham-Noodle Pancake is a crispy skillet dish that's perfect for brunch. Pasta Fajitas and Mexican Pasta with Beef are new ways to enjoy south-of-the-border cuisine. And especially for seafood lovers, we've included Greek Pasta with Shrimp, Ginger Scallops with Chinese Noodles and Shrimp Wontons.

Chinese Spicy Beans and Pasta

111

Makes 4 servings

If you can't find Chinese long green beans, try this dish with green or pole beans. If you like things extra-spicy, increase the garlic and red pepper flakes.

4 cups (¾ pound) Chinese long green beans, trimmed
½ teaspoon salt
6 ounces perciatelli (long tubular macaroni), cooked and drained

2 tablespoons dark sesame oil
1 cup red bell pepper, cut into strips
3 garlic cloves, minced
½ cup chicken broth
½ teaspoon dried red pepper flakes

1. In large pot of rapidly boiling water, cook beans with salt 5-7 minutes, until just tender. Remove beans with tongs; place in large serving bowl with perciatelli; cover with foil.

2. In medium nonstick skillet, heat oil; sauté bell pepper and garlic 5 minutes, stirring occasionally. Add remaining ingredients; simmer 3-5 minutes. Pour over beans and perciatelli; toss to coat.

EACH SERVING PROVIDES: 1½ FATS; 2½ VEGETABLES; 2 BREADS; 5 OPTIONAL CALORIES.
PER SERVING: 272 CALORIES; 9 G PROTEIN; 8 G FAT; 41 G CARBOHYDRATE; 404 MG SODIUM;
0 MG CHOLESTEROL; 1 G DIETARY FIBER.

REDUCED FAT; CHOLESTEROL-FREE

Pork Lo Mein

Makes 4 servings

Crunchy and flavorful with sesame and peanut oil, our version is full of all the goodies that make this Chinese take-out favorite famous.

10 ounces boneless lean pork, cut into ¼" strips
1 large egg white, slightly beaten
2 tablespoons low-sodium soy sauce
1 tablespoon rice wine vinegar
16 small dried Oriental mushrooms*
1 tablespoon peanut oil
2 teaspoons grated fresh ginger
⅛ teaspoon dried red pepper flakes
1 cup shredded bok choy

1 cup thinly sliced green bell pepper
½ cup thinly sliced red bell pepper
½ cup diced pared jicama
¼ teaspoon garlic powder
1 tablespoon cornstarch
3 ounces whole-wheat or buckwheat soba* spaghetti, cooked and drained
1 teaspoon sesame oil

1. Spray broiler rack with nonstick cooking spray. Preheat broiler; broil pork strips 4" from heat, 2 minutes.

2. In small bowl, combine pork, egg white, soy sauce and vinegar. Let stand 30 minutes.

3. In small bowl, combine dried mushrooms with ½ cup warm water; set aside.

4. In large nonstick skillet, heat peanut oil; add ginger and pepper flakes. Cook, stirring constantly, 2 minutes. Add pork mixture; cook, stirring frequently, 2 minutes.

5. With slotted spoon, remove mushrooms from bowl; reserve liquid. Add mushrooms, bok choy, bell pepper, jicama and garlic powder to skillet; cook, stirring, 3-4 minutes, until vegetables are tender.

6. Dissolve cornstarch in reserved mushroom liquid. Add cornstarch mixture, spaghetti and sesame oil to skillet. Cook 1-2 minutes, tossing well, or until liquid has thickened.

*Available at Asian markets; mushrooms may be found in produce sections of some supermarkets.

EACH SERVING PROVIDES: 1 FAT; 2 PROTEINS; 2 VEGETABLES; 1 BREAD; 15 OPTIONAL CALORIES.
PER SERVING: 279 CALORIES; 20 G PROTEIN; 10 G FAT; 28 G CARBOHYDRATE; 273 MG SODIUM;
46 MG CHOLESTEROL; 3 G DIETARY FIBER.

REDUCED FAT, SODIUM AND CHOLESTEROL

Ginger Scallops with Chinese Noodles

113

Makes 4 servings

Delicate angel hair pasta gets coated with this richly flavored sauce. Store extra fresh ginger in a small glass jar of dry sherry, covered and refrigerated. Slice and use as needed.

1/4 cup minced scallions
1/4 cup low-sodium chicken broth
2 tablespoons dry white wine
1 teaspoon cornstarch
1/4 teaspoon granulated sugar
1/8 teaspoon ground white pepper
2 garlic cloves, minced

1/4 teaspoon salt
2 3/4 cups cut fresh green beans
1 teaspoon sesame oil
2 teaspoons grated fresh ginger
10 ounces sea or bay scallops
3 ounces angel hair pasta, cooked
   and drained

1. In small bowl, combine scallions, broth, wine, cornstarch, sugar and pepper; set aside.

2. Spray large nonstick skillet or wok with nonstick cooking spray; heat over medium-high heat. Add garlic and salt; stir-fry 1-2 minutes, until garlic is tender. Add beans; stir-fry 3 minutes. Add 1/3 cup water and continue cooking 3-4 minutes, until tender. Remove bean mixture to medium bowl.

3. Heat sesame oil in same skillet; add ginger; stir-fry 2 minutes. Add scallops; stir-fry 5-6 minutes, until scallops turn opaque. Add beans and scallion mixture to skillet; heat 1-2 minutes, until mixture thickens and coats scallops. Place pasta in serving bowl; add scallop mixture; toss to mix well.

EACH SERVING PROVIDES: 1 FAT; 1 PROTEIN; 1 1/2 VEGETABLES; 1 BREAD; 10 OPTIONAL CALORIES.
PER SERVING: 194 CALORIES; 16 G PROTEIN; 3 G FAT; 25 G CARBOHYDRATE; 259 MG SODIUM;
23 MG CHOLESTEROL; 2 G DIETARY FIBER.

REDUCED FAT AND CHOLESTEROL

Spicy Hunan Sesame Noodles

Makes 4 servings

The exotic ingredients are well worth the trip to an Asian or specialty foods market. Stock up because you'll want to make this dish again! You can substitute peanut butter for the tahini.

1 garlic clove
One 1x1¼" piece ginger root, pared
¼ cup tahini (sesame seed paste)
3 tablespoons brewed black tea
2 tablespoons low-sodium soy sauce
2 teaspoons honey
¼-½ teaspoon garlic chili paste*

4 cups cooked spaghetti squash
3 ounces spaghetti, cooked and drained
1 cup thinly sliced red bell pepper
½ cup thinly sliced scallions
8 ounces drained rinsed cooked cannellini beans

1. In food processor, mince garlic and ginger. Add tahini, tea, soy sauce, honey and chili paste; process until smooth.

2. In large bowl, combine spaghetti squash, spaghetti, pepper and scallions; add tahini mixture and beans, tossing until combined. Serve warm or chilled.

*Available at Asian markets.

EACH SERVING PROVIDES: 1 FAT; 2 PROTEINS; 1 BREAD; 2³/₄ VEGETABLES; 10 OPTIONAL CALORIES.
PER SERVING: 330 CALORIES; 12 G PROTEIN; 10 G FAT; 51 G CARBOHYDRATE; 364 MG SODIUM;
0 MG CHOLESTEROL; 7 G DIETARY FIBER.

REDUCED FAT AND SODIUM; CHOLESTEROL-FREE

Makes 4 servings

Thin, transparent cellophane noodles, made from powdered mung beans, are the perfect pasta to absorb all the flavors in this dish, but you can also use fettuccine or tagliatelle.

1 tablespoon + 1 teaspoon wine vinegar

1 tablespoon + 1 teaspoon olive or canola oil

8 dried tomato halves, soaked in boiling water, drained and diced

1 tablespoon + 1 teaspoon rinsed capers

3 ounces cellophane noodles, cooked and drained

2 cups blanched broccoli florets

1 cup shredded carrots

8 ounces smoked lean ham, cut into thin strips

In medium bowl, combine vinegar, oil, tomatoes and capers. Stir in noodles, broccoli, carrots and ham. Toss to mix well.

EACH SERVING PROVIDES: 1 FAT; 2½ PROTEINS; 2 VEGETABLES; 1 BREAD
PER SERVING: 229 CALORIES; 14 G PROTEIN; 8 G FAT; 27 G CARBOHYDRATE; 915 MG SODIUM;
27 MG CHOLESTEROL; 1 G DIETARY FIBER.

REDUCED CHOLESTEROL

Thai-Style Noodles

Makes 4 servings

Sweet and spicy, these peanutty noodles get a kick from scallions and cilantro. A simple grilled chicken kabob and a crunchy salad with bean sprouts are excellent accompaniments.

3 tablespoons natural peanut butter
2 tablespoons chicken broth or water
1 tablespoon soy sauce
2 teaspoons finely chopped fresh lemongrass* (optional)
2 teaspoons sesame oil
2 teaspoons honey
1½ teaspoons finely chopped garlic
1½ teaspoons finely chopped fresh ginger

¼ teaspoon chili oil or sesame hot oil (or more to taste)*
6 ounces spaghetti, cooked, drained and rinsed in cold water
¼ cup chopped scallions (white part only)
2 teaspoons chopped fresh cilantro
½ ounce chopped dry roasted peanuts to garnish (optional)**

1. To prepare sauce, combine peanut butter, broth, soy sauce, lemongrass, sesame oil, honey, garlic, ginger and chili oil in blender or food processor; puree until smooth.

2. In large serving bowl, toss spaghetti with the sauce, half the scallions and half the cilantro. Garnish with remaining scallions, cilantro and the coarsely chopped peanuts, if using.

*Available at Asian markets.

EACH SERVING PROVIDES: 1¼ FATS; ¾ PROTEIN; 2 BREADS; 15 OPTIONAL CALORIES.
PER SERVING: 274 CALORIES; 9 G PROTEIN; 9 G FAT; 38 G CARBOHYDRATE; 339 MG SODIUM;
0 MG CHOLESTEROL; 1 G DIETARY FIBER.
**ADD ¼ FAT; 10 CALORIES PER SERVING IF USING.

CHOLESTEROL-FREE

117 Buckwheat Soba with Grilled Eggplant

Makes 4 servings

Make this part of your summer barbecue and grill the eggplant slices outdoors. This exotic dish from Japan is bound to be a conversation starter.

¼ cup chicken broth or water
2½ tablespoons light miso paste (Shiro)*
1½ teaspoons finely chopped garlic
1½ teaspoons finely chopped fresh ginger
2 teaspoons sesame oil
1 teaspoon tamari soy sauce*
½ teaspoon chili oil or sesame hot oil*
3 small Japanese or Italian eggplants, cut lengthwise into ¼" slices

6 ounces buckwheat soba noodles*, cooked, drained and rinsed in cold water
2 teaspoons chopped fresh flat-leaf parsley
2 teaspoons chopped fresh cilantro
¼ cup chopped scallions (white part only)
1 teaspoon sesame seeds

1. Preheat stovetop grill, or prepare outdoor grill, following manufacturer's directions.

2. To prepare sauce, in small bowl, whisk broth and miso, mixing until smooth (add a teaspoon water, if necessary, to achieve smooth consistency). Add garlic, ginger, sesame oil, soy sauce and chili oil; whisk thoroughly.

3. Grill eggplant slices until well browned on both sides, turning occasionally. Cut each slice lengthwise into ¹/8" thin julienne strips. Transfer to large serving bowl; pour sauce over eggplant and toss to coat.

4. Add soba noodles, half the parsley and cilantro and 3 tablespoons of the scallions; toss to combine. Garnish with the remaining parsley, cilantro, scallions and the sesame seeds.

* Available at Asian markets and some health-food stores.

EACH SERVING PROVIDES: ¹/2 FAT; 3 VEGETABLES; 2 BREADS; 25 OPTIONAL CALORIES.
PER SERVING: 246 CALORIES; 10 G PROTEIN; 4 G FAT; 47 G CARBOHYDRATE; 883 MG SODIUM;
0 MG CHOLESTEROL; 3 G DIETARY FIBER.

REDUCED FAT; CHOLESTEROL-FREE

Shrimp Wontons

Makes 4 servings

Steaming bowls of chicken broth seasoned with soy sauce are perfect to float these shrimp-filled wontons, the Oriental cousin to ravioli.

8 ounces cooked shelled deveined shrimp
2 egg whites
2 scallions (white parts only), finely chopped (reserve greens for garnish)
Pinch salt
Freshly ground white pepper to taste
½ teaspoon finely chopped fresh ginger
½ teaspoon finely chopped garlic
20 wonton skins (3" squares)
1 tablespoon tamari soy sauce*

1. To prepare filling, chop shrimp; place in medium bowl. Stir in 1 egg white, scallions, salt, white pepper to taste, scallions, ginger and garlic.

2. To assemble wontons, place wonton skins on work surface. Place 1 teaspoonful of filling in the center of each skin. Brush edges with remaining egg white and fold diagonally to form a triangle. Press edges to seal, pressing out air. Leave wontons as triangles or join the two bottom points, one over the other, sealing with egg white.

3. In large pot of boiling water, cook wontons 1 minute. Remove with slotted spoon to serving bowl; sprinkle evenly with soy sauce.

*Available at Asian markets and some health-food stores.

EACH SERVING PROVIDES: 1 PROTEIN; 1 BREAD; 10 OPTIONAL CALORIES.
PER SERVING: 157 CALORIES; 18 G PROTEIN; 1 G FAT; 18 G CARBOHYDRATE; 449 MG SODIUM; 111 MG CHOLESTEROL; 0 G DIETARY FIBER.

REDUCED FAT

Thai-Style Ravioli

Makes 4 servings

These shrimp-filled wontons are cooked in broth and served with a sassy cilantro-duck sauce. Make them a surprise first course or part of an international buffet.

1 tablespoon + 1 teaspoon canola or vegetable oil
1 cup coarsely chopped bok choy (Chinese cabbage)
1/4 cup coarsely shredded carrot
12 shelled deveined cooked shrimp, cut into 1/4" pieces
1/2 cup coarsely chopped bean sprouts
2 tablespoons + 1 teaspoon finely chopped fresh cilantro

2 tablespoons finely chopped scallions
3 tablespoons finely chopped water chestnuts
1/2 teaspoon grated fresh ginger
1 teaspoon low-sodium soy sauce
1 teaspoon cornstarch
20 wonton skins (3" squares)
1 1/2 cups low-sodium chicken broth
3 tablespoons duck sauce
1 tablespoon rice wine vinegar

1. In large nonstick skillet, heat oil; add bok choy and carrot. Cook over medium-high heat, stirring constantly, until cabbage is wilted and bright green, about 2 minutes. Add shrimp, bean sprouts, 2 tablespoons of the cilantro, the scallions, water chestnuts and ginger; cook, stirring, 1 minute longer. Add soy sauce and cornstarch; mix thoroughly. Let cool slightly.

2. Arrange 10 wonton skins on work surface. Spoon equal amounts (about 1 tablespoon) of the cabbage mixture in center of each skin. Moisten edges of skins with water; place remaining 10 skins over filling. Using tines of fork, press edges firmly to seal.

3. In same skillet, bring broth to a boil. Place ravioli in broth; reduce heat to low and simmer, covered, 5 minutes.

4. Meanwhile, in small bowl, combine duck sauce, rice wine vinegar and the remaining 1 teaspoon cilantro. Spoon ravioli and any remaining broth into shallow serving bowl; serve with sauce.

EACH SERVING PROVIDES: 1 FAT; 1/2 PROTEIN; 3/4 VEGETABLE; 1 1/4 BREAD; 25 OPTIONAL CALORIES.
PER SERVING: 188 CALORIES; 12 G PROTEIN; 6 G FAT; 23 G CARBOHYDRATE; 141 MG SODIUM;
35 MG CHOLESTEROL; 0 G DIETARY FIBER.

REDUCED FAT AND SODIUM

120 Potstickers

Makes 4 servings

These wonton packages get their name because of their tendency to adhere to the skillet when cooking. You may recognize them as the dumplings offered on most Chinese takeout menus. We've included a recipe for dipping sauce.

FILLING:
8 ounces ground pork, broiled
   2 minutes
¼ cup minced scallions
3 tablespoons minced water chestnuts
2 teaspoons minced fresh ginger
1 tablespoon Chinese rice wine or dry
   sherry
2 teaspoons low-sodium soy sauce
1 teaspoon sesame oil

1 egg white
20 wonton skins (3" squares)
1 tablespoon + 1 teaspoons canola or
   vegetable oil

DIPPING SAUCE:
2 tablespoons low-sodium soy sauce
2 tablespoons rice wine vinegar
½ teaspoon sesame oil
1 teaspoon minced scallion

1. In food processor, combine all filling ingredients except wonton skins and canola oil; process until just combined.

2. Arrange wonton skins on work surface. Spoon an equal amount of filling on the center of each skin; lightly moisten edges with water. Bring top and bottom corners of skin over filling and pinch to seal, then bring the two other corners together to meet in center. Press all edges to seal securely.

3. In large nonstick skillet, heat canola oil. Arrange filled wontons in skillet in a closely packed circle, sealed side up. Cook over medium-high heat until edges begin to brown, about 5 minutes; carefully pour ¹/2 cup water into skillet (watch for splattering); immediately cover skillet. Reduce heat to medium; cook 15 minutes. Increase heat to medium-high; cook, uncovered, until undersides are crisp, about 5 minutes. Loosen with a spatula.

4. Meanwhile, in small bowl, combine all dipping sauce ingredients. Serve with potstickers.

EACH SERVING (5 POTSTICKERS) PROVIDES: 1¹/2 FATS; 1¹/2 PROTEINS; 1¹/4 BREADS; 15 OPTIONAL CALORIES.
PER SERVING: 329 CALORIES; 14 G PROTEIN; 21 G FAT; 21 G CARBOHYDRATE; 318 MG SODIUM;
41 MG CHOLESTEROL; 0 G DIETARY FIBER.

121 Linguine a la Greque

Makes 4 servings

This dish sounds exotic, but uses ordinary ingredients you'll find in your own pantry and freezer. Ripe tomatoes with crumbled feta cheese and oregano would be a tasty side dish.

2 cups frozen chopped spinach
  (one 10-ounce package)
8 ounces drained cooked chick-peas
¼ cup golden raisins
6 ounces linguine, cooked and drained

½ teaspoon salt
⅛ teaspoon crushed red pepper
  flakes
1 tablespoon + 1 teaspoon olive oil

1. In medium saucepan, cook spinach, following package directions. Add chick-peas and raisins; cook, stirring occasionally, until heated through.

2. In large bowl, combine spinach mixture with pasta; sprinkle with salt and red pepper. Drizzle with oil; toss to combine.

EACH SERVING PROVIDES: 1 FAT; 1 PROTEIN; 1 VEGETABLE; 2 BREADS; ½ FRUIT.
PER SERVING: 311 CALORIES; 11 G PROTEIN; 7 G FAT; 52 G CARBOHYDRATE; 442 MG SODIUM;
0 MG CHOLESTEROL; 6 G DIETARY FIBER.

REDUCED FAT; CHOLESTEROL-FREE

Greek Lasagna

Makes 6 servings

Try this dish with spinach or whole-wheat lasagna noodles if available; serve with crusty bread and a big Greek salad for an easy party meal.

1¼ cups part-skim ricotta cheese
9 ounces drained soft tofu
3 ounces crumbled feta cheese
6 cups undrained thawed frozen
   chopped spinach (three 10-ounce
   packages)
1 cup thinly sliced scallions
2 tablespoons chopped fresh dill

½ teaspoon salt
¼ teaspoon ground nutmeg
¼ teaspoon freshly ground black
   pepper
9 ounces curly or plain lasagna
   noodles, cooked and drained
   (9 noodles)
2 medium tomatoes, thinly sliced

1. In food processor, puree ricotta, tofu and feta until smooth.

2. In large bowl, combine spinach, scallions, dill, salt, nutmeg and pepper; add cheese mixture and mix well.

3. Preheat oven to 350°F. Spray a 13x9" baking pan with nonstick cooking spray. Arrange one-third of the lasagna noodles in prepared pan; top with half the spinach mixture. Repeat layering, ending with a noodle layer; top evenly with tomatoes. Bake 30 minutes. Let stand 10 minutes before serving.

EACH SERVING PROVIDES: 2 PROTEINS; 3 VEGETABLES; 2 BREADS.
PER SERVING: 339 CALORIES; 20 G PROTEIN; 9 G FAT; 45 G CARBOHYDRATE; 521 MG SODIUM;
28 MG CHOLESTEROL; 5 G DIETARY FIBER.

REDUCED FAT AND CHOLESTEROL

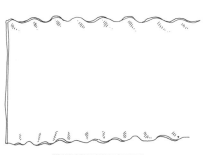

123 Lamb with Orzo

Makes 4 servings

Lamb, yogurt, mint, lemon—staples of Mediterranean cooking—are combined with zucchini and served on a bed of orzo for a quick weeknight meal.

10 ounces boneless lean lamb,
   cut into 1" cubes
2 teaspoons olive oil
½ cup chopped onion
1½ cups thinly sliced zucchini
2 tablespoons chopped fresh mint

¼ teaspoon salt
½ cup plain lowfat yogurt
2 tablespoons lemon juice
3 ounces orzo, cooked and
   drained

1. Preheat broiler; broil lamb cubes on rack 4" from heat, 2 minutes.

2. In medium nonstick skillet, heat olive oil; add onion. Cook, stirring frequently, 2-3 minutes, until tender. Add lamb cubes, zucchini, mint and salt; cook, stirring frequently, 5-6 minutes, until zucchini is tender and lamb is done to taste.

3. Remove lamb mixture from heat; stir in yogurt and lemon juice. Spoon lamb mixture over orzo. Toss to mix well.

EACH SERVING PROVIDES: ¼ MILK; ½ FAT; 2 PROTEINS; 1 BREAD; 1 VEGETABLE.
PER SERVING: 227 CALORIES; 19 G PROTEIN; 7 G FAT; 21 G CARBOHYDRATE; 207 MG SODIUM;
48 MG CHOLESTEROL;1 G DIETARY FIBER.

REDUCED FAT, SODIUM AND CHOLESTEROL

Greek Pasta with Shrimp

Makes 4 servings

A classic dish served in the isles of Greece. A simple salad, crusty bread to scoop up the tomato and feta sauce and a hearty Greek wine are the makings of a memorable meal.

12 fresh or frozen medium shrimp	1 teaspoon dried oregano
2 teaspoons olive oil	½ teaspoon dried tarragon
1 tablespoon rinsed drained capers	1½ ounces feta cheese, crumbled
2 garlic cloves, minced	3 ounces orzo, cooked and drained
1 cup chopped drained canned tomatoes	

1. Shell and devein shrimp, leaving tail section on.

2. In large nonstick skillet, heat olive oil; add capers and garlic. Sauté 1-2 minutes, until garlic is tender.

3. Add shrimp, tomatoes, oregano and tarragon. Sauté 5-6 minutes, stirring constantly, until shrimp become pink and opaque. Remove skillet from heat; stir in feta cheese. Spoon shrimp over orzo; toss to mix well.

EACH SERVING PROVIDES: ½ FAT; 1 PROTEIN; ½ VEGETABLE; 1 BREAD.
PER SERVING: 173 CALORIES; 11 G PROTEIN; 6 G FAT; 20 G CARBOHYDRATE; 315 MG SODIUM;
53 MG CHOLESTEROL; 1 G DIETARY FIBER.

German Ham and Noodle Pancake

Makes 4 servings

Crispy brown noodles and ham have a baked taste, although they are made in a skillet. Serve with cole slaw and light beer.

2 teaspoons sesame oil
1 cup chopped scallions
4½ ounces wide egg noodles, cooked and drained

4 ounces cubed cooked ham
1 cup egg substitute
¼ cup chopped fresh parsley
Freshly ground black pepper to taste

1. In large nonstick skillet, heat oil; add scallions. Cook, stirring frequently, 5-7 minutes, until tender. Add noodles; cook 1 minute, stirring to coat with oil. Stir in ham.

2. Pour egg substitute over noodle mixture. Place a large heatproof plate on top of noodle mixture; press down firmly. Cook 5 minutes, until crust forms on bottom. With spatula, cut noodle "pancake" in sections and turn carefully. Press top firmly with plate and cook 2-3 minutes longer, until bottom is browned and crisp. Sprinkle with parsley and pepper to taste; serve immediately.

EACH SERVING PROVIDES: 1/2 FAT; 2 PROTEINS; 1/2 VEGETABLE; 11/2 BREADS.

PER SERVING: 217 CALORIES; 16 G PROTEIN; 5 G FAT; 26 G CARBOHYDRATE; 433 MG SODIUM; 45 MG CHOLESTEROL; 2 G DIETARY FIBER.

REDUCED FAT AND CHOLESTEROL

Spaetzle with Paprika Sauce

Makes 4 servings

You don't need a machine to make this homemade pasta indigenous to Germany and Austria. Use the best quality Hungarian paprika available for optimum flavor. Make some extra spaetzle to use for soup.

SAUCE:
1 tablespoon + 1 teaspoon canola oil
2 large red bell peppers, thinly sliced
½ cup finely chopped onion
½ cup finely chopped celery
2 cups canned Italian tomatoes, chopped
2 teaspoons paprika
1 tablespoon part-skim ricotta cheese, at room temperature
Freshly ground black pepper to taste

SPAETZLE:
2 eggs
1½ cups all-purpose flour
½ teaspoon salt, or to taste
Freshly ground black pepper to taste
Pinch ground nutmeg
½ teaspoon baking powder
2 tablespoons grated Parmesan cheese

1. To prepare sauce, in large nonstick skillet, heat oil; add bell peppers, onion and celery. Sauté, stirring, 10 minutes. Add tomatoes, paprika and 2 tablespoons water. Cover and cook over low heat, stirring occasionally, 1 hour, until peppers are completely tender.

2. Press pepper mixture through the medium disk of a food mill into large bowl. Mix in ricotta; season with black pepper to taste.

3. To prepare spaetzle, bring a large pot of water to a boil. In medium bowl, beat eggs; add flour, ¹/2 cup water, salt, black pepper to taste, nutmeg and baking powder, stirring until smooth. Reduce heat under water to a simmer.

4. Using 2 teaspoons, drop very small amounts (approximately ¹/2 teaspoon) of batter into simmering water. Cook 3 minutes (spaetzle will float to surface). Remove with a slotted spoon; add pepper mixture; toss to coat well. Sprinkle evenly with Parmesan cheese.

EACH SERVING PROVIDES: 1 FAT; ¹/2 PROTEIN; 2¹/2 VEGETABLES; 2 BREADS; 20 OPTIONAL CALORIES.
PER SERVING: 324 CALORIES; 12 G PROTEIN; 9 G FAT; 50 G CARBOHYDRATE; 622 MG SODIUM;
109 MG CHOLESTEROL; 4 G DIETARY FIBER.

REDUCED FAT

127 Pappardelle with Savoy Cabbage

Makes 4 servings

In Northern Italy, pappardelle is often served with rabbit sauce. These short, wide noodles are also a hearty match for roast lamb or pork. For a variation, when sautéing cabbage, add a teaspoon of caraway seeds.

2 teaspoons canola oil
2 teaspoons extra virgin olive oil
1½ cups very thinly sliced red onion
2 teaspoons chopped fresh rosemary
1 pound savoy cabbage (1 small head), cored and thinly sliced or shredded
Salt and freshly ground black pepper to taste

1 cup chicken broth
1 teaspoon butter-flavored granules (optional)*
6 ounces pappardelle or fettuccine, cooked and drained
2 tablespoons grated Parmesan cheese
1 tablespoon finely chopped fresh flat-leaf parsley

1. In large heavy saucepan, heat oil; add onion and rosemary. Sauté, stirring, until onion is translucent, 2 minutes. Add cabbage, salt and pepper to taste and ½ cup of the broth; cook, stirring, until cabbage is wilted and liquid is evaporated. Add the remaining ½ cup broth; cover and simmer 30-40 minutes, until cabbage is tender, stirring occasionally.

2. Uncover, increase heat to high and stir until excess liquid is evaporated. Add butter granules, if using. Transfer mixture to large serving bowl.

3. Add pasta to cabbage; sprinkle with Parmesan cheese and toss to coat. Sprinkle with parsley.

EACH SERVING PROVIDES: 1 FAT; 3³/₄ VEGETABLES; 2 BREADS; 25 OPTIONAL CALORIES.
PER SERVING: 266 CALORIES; 10 G PROTEIN; 7 G FAT; 43 G CARBOHYDRATE; 328 MG SODIUM;
2 MG CHOLESTEROL; 1 G DIETARY FIBER.
*ADD 2 CALORIES PER SERVING IF USING.

REDUCED FAT AND CHOLESTEROL

128 Pasta Jambalaya

Makes 4 servings

Pasta with a Cajun touch—chicken, shrimp and sausage in one dish!

2 teaspoons olive oil
4 ounces hot Italian turkey sausage, cut into ¼" pieces
4 ounces boneless skinless chicken breast, cut into 1" pieces
12 medium shrimp, shelled and deveined
1 cup sliced green bell pepper
½ cup chopped onion
1 garlic clove, minced

1½ cups canned crushed tomatoes
¼ cup clam juice
¼ cup low-sodium chicken broth
¼ teaspoon dried basil
⅛ teaspoon garlic powder
⅛ teaspoon salt
Dash ground red pepper
6 ounces fresh or dried spinach fettuccine, cooked and drained

1. In large nonstick skillet, heat oil; add sausage. Cook, stirring frequently, 6-8 minutes, until browned. Add chicken; cook, stirring frequently, 5 minutes. Stir in shrimp; cook 5 minutes longer, or until chicken is browned and shrimp are pink and opaque. With slotted spoon, remove sausage, chicken and shrimp to plate.

2. Add bell pepper, onion and garlic to skillet; cook, stirring frequently, 3 minutes, until tender. Stir in tomatoes and remaining ingredients except fettuccine. Bring to a boil; add sausage, chicken and shrimp. Reduce heat to low; simmer 15 minutes.

3. Transfer to large serving bowl. Add fettuccine; toss to combine.

EACH SERVING PROVIDES: ¹/₂ FAT; 2 PROTEINS; 1¹/₂ VEGETABLES; 2 BREADS; 5 OPTIONAL CALORIES.
PER SERVING: 288 CALORIES; 25 G PROTEIN; 8 G FAT; 30 G CARBOHYDRATE; 502 MG SODIUM;
131 MG CHOLESTEROL; 1 G DIETARY FIBER.

REDUCED FAT

Shrimp Creole Lasagna

Makes 4 servings

This spicy twist on traditional lasagna brings the bayou to your kitchen!

2 teaspoons olive oil
½ cup finely chopped celery
½ cup finely chopped onion
½ cup finely chopped yellow or
   green bell pepper
1 tablespoon all-purpose flour
1 teaspoon Creole seasoning
2 cups canned low-sodium crushed
   tomatoes

½ cup sliced okra
1 bay leaf
1 ⅓ cups low-fat (1%) cottage cheese
3 ounces crumbled feta cheese
1 tablespoon egg substitute
4 ounces lasagna noodles, cooked
   and drained (4 noodles)
18 medium shrimp, shelled and
   deveined

1. In large saucepan, heat oil; add celery, onion and bell pepper. Cook over medium-high heat, stirring, until onion is translucent, about 3 minutes. Add flour and Creole seasoning; toss to coat vegetables; cook 1 minute longer. Stir in tomatoes, okra, ¼ cup water and bay leaf; bring to a boil. Reduce heat to low; simmer, covered, 5 minutes. Uncover and simmer 5 minutes longer, stirring occasionally, until mixture is very thick. Remove bay leaf.

2. Preheat oven to 350°F. In small bowl, combine cottage cheese, feta and egg substitute, mixing well. Spread mixture evenly over lasagna noodles; roll up jelly-roll style.

3. Spread ½ cup sauce (without okra) in bottom of a 10" round or 8" square baking pan. Place lasagna rolls seam-side down in pan; spoon remaining sauce over top. Cover with foil; bake 30 minutes. Uncover and arrange shrimp on top. Bake, covered, until shrimp turn pink, 5-7 minutes.

EACH SERVING PROVIDES: ½ FAT; 3 PROTEINS; 2 VEGETABLES; 1¼ BREADS; 15 OPTIONAL CALORIES.
PER SERVING: 335 CALORIES; 27 G PROTEIN; 9 G FAT; 36 G CARBOHYDRATE; 854 MG SODIUM;
87 MG CHOLESTEROL; 3 G DIETARY FIBER.

REDUCED FAT

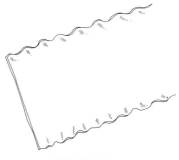

Spanish Pasta with Sardines and Saffron

Makes 4 servings

Turn those cans of sardines in your pantry into something special! Saffron provides vivid color, while fresh fennel and pine nuts add texture and taste.

1 cup diced fennel
2 teaspoons olive oil
1 cup chopped onion
3 ounces drained sardines
4 ounces (½ cup) dry white wine
⅛ teaspoon powdered saffron

⅛ teaspoon freshly ground black
  pepper
½ ounce toasted pignolias (pine nuts)
6 pitted large black olives, quartered
3 ounces linguine
Fresh fennel leaves for garnish

1. In large pot of boiling water, cook fennel 10 minutes. Remove to bowl with slotted spoon; reserve liquid in pot.

2. In medium nonstick skillet, heat oil; add onion. Sauté, stirring frequently, until tender, about 4 minutes. Add sardines and fennel; cook over low heat 5 minutes, stirring occasionally.

3. Add wine, ¹/2 cup of the reserved fennel cooking liquid, the saffron, pepper, pine nuts and olives. Simmer 10 minutes, stirring frequently.

4. Meanwhile, return the fennel cooking liquid to a boil; add linguine and cook 9-10 minutes, until tender; drain and place in serving bowl.

5. To serve, toss linguine with sardine mixture. Garnish with fresh fennel leaves.

EACH SERVING PROVIDES: 1 FAT; ¹/2 PROTEIN; 1 VEGETABLE; 1 BREAD; 25 OPTIONAL CALORIES.
PER SERVING: 209 CALORIES; 10 G PROTEIN; 8 G FAT; 21 G CARBOHYDRATE; 201 MG SODIUM;
30 MG CHOLESTEROL; 2 G DIETARY FIBER.

Mexican Pasta with Beef

Makes 8 servings

This exotic dish pairs sweet and savory for a unique taste sensation. You can substitute lean ground turkey for the beef.

1 tablespoon + 1 teaspoon olive oil
1 pound 3 ounces lean ground beef,
　broiled 2 minutes
1 cup chopped red onion
1 cup evaporated skimmed milk
1 cup thinly sliced red bell pepper
¼ cup golden raisins

1 ounce sliced natural almonds
1 tablespoon chopped fresh mint
¼ teaspoon ground cinnamon
¼ teaspoon salt
6 ounces tricolored rotelle,
　cooked and drained

1. In large nonstick skillet, heat oil; add beef and onion. Cook, stirring to break up beef, 2-3 minutes, until beef is no longer pink.

2. Stir in milk, pepper, raisins, almonds, mint, cinnamon and salt. Cook, stirring frequently, 8-10 minutes, until most of the liquid has evaporated.

3. Combine meat mixture and rotelle in large serving bowl; toss to mix well.

EACH SERVING PROVIDES: ¼ MILK; ¾ FAT; 2 PROTEINS; ½ VEGETABLE; 1 BREAD; ¼ FRUIT.
PER SERVING: 315 CALORIES; 20 G PROTEIN; 15 G FAT; 26 G CARBOHYDRATE; 158 MG SODIUM;
48 MG CHOLESTEROL; 2 G DIETARY FIBER.

REDUCED SODIUM AND CHOLESTEROL

Pasta Fajitas

Makes 2 servings

Manicotti shells stand in for flour tortillas in this dish, inspired by the popular Mexican standard. Serve with a relish tray—spicy salsa, chopped jalapeño peppers, red onions, cilantro—and top with dollops of plain nonfat yogurt.

¼ teaspoon grated lime peel
¼ cup + ¼ teaspoon fresh lime juice
1 garlic clove, minced
¼ teaspoon salt
¼ teaspoon ground cumin
6 ounces turkey cutlets, cut into
   1" strips
½ cup sliced red bell pepper

½ cup sliced green bell pepper
½ cup slivered onion
2 ounces cubed avocado
2 tablespoons plain nonfat yogurt
3 ounces manicotti shells, cooked and
   drained (about 4)
½ cup shredded lettuce

1. In shallow 11x7" glass dish, combine lime peel and ¼ cup of the lime juice, the garlic, salt and cumin. Add turkey strips; toss to coat. Push to one side; add red and green peppers and onion; toss to coat, but do not combine with turkey. Cover and marinate in refrigerator 1 hour.

2. Preheat broiler. Line a baking sheet with foil; spray foil with nonstick cooking spray.

3. With slotted spoon, transfer turkey and vegetables to prepared baking sheet. Broil, turning once, until turkey is cooked through and vegetables are softened, about 2-3 minutes.

4. Meanwhile, in small bowl, mash together the avocado, yogurt and ¼ teaspoon of the lime juice; set aside.

5. Slit manicotti shells lengthwise; open flat. Divide turkey and vegetables evenly among each manicotti; top evenly with the avocado mixture and lettuce. To eat, wrap manicotti around filling (like a taco).

EACH SERVING PROVIDES: 1 FAT; 2 PROTEINS; 2 VEGETABLES; 2 BREADS; 10 OPTIONAL CALORIES.
PER SERVING: 356 CALORIES; 29 G PROTEIN; 7 G FAT; 46 G CARBOHYDRATE; 333 MG SODIUM;
53 MG CHOLESTEROL; 3 G DIETARY FIBER.

REDUCED FAT AND SODIUM

Microwave

The microwave has revolutionized the way we cook and, for some folks, has even replaced the conventional oven. Speed is not the only advantage. Microwave cooking tends to be lighter, since you can use less fat and still retain the tender juiciness of foods as well as preserve vitamins and nutrients. Orzo, angel hair, thin spaghetti, couscous and small pastas can actually be cooked in the microwave, while larger, heartier shapes need to be prepared the traditional way. To take advantage of microwave convenience, you can boil and drain pasta, measure serving sizes and freeze in sealable plastic bags. This way, you'll always have cooked pasta ready for a microwave recipe. All the recipes in this chapter were tested in a 700-watt microwave oven, using microwave safe utensils, and many use convenience products to make preparation even faster. If your microwave does not have a turntable, you may need to rotate food while cooking, as well as stir foods several times during cooking. If you need to elevate food when cooking, place the dish on a plastic microwave rack or inverted glass pie plate. Then, enjoy the pleasures of this chapter: Orzo Pilaf, easy microwave Meat Sauce, Fusilli with Red Clam Sauce, Curried Chicken with Couscous and Chicken Chinoise with Angel Hair are only a few great ideas for a speedy special meal. There's no limit to your microwave pastabilities!

134 Manhattan-Style Clam Chowder

Makes 4 servings

There's nothing better than being able to whip up a quick, satisfying soup in the microwave, especially when pasta is cooked right along with it.

½ cup minced carrot
½ cup chopped celery
½ cup chopped onion
½ cup chopped green bell pepper
1 cup clam juice
2 cups canned tomatoes

1½ ounces small pasta shells
½ teaspoon dried oregano
⅛ teaspoon freshly ground black pepper
8 ounces fresh or drained canned whole small clams

1. In a 2½-quart casserole, combine carrot, celery, onion, bell pepper and ½ cup of the clam juice. Microwave, covered, on High 7-8 minutes, until vegetables are tender, stirring halfway through cooking.

2. Add tomatoes with their liquid, breaking up tomatoes with spoon, pasta shells, oregano, pepper and the remaining ½ cup clam juice. Microwave, covered, on High 10-12 minutes, until shells are tender, stirring halfway through cooking.

3. Stir in clams; microwave, covered, on High 1 minute, just until clams are heated through.

EACH SERVING (ABOUT 1 CUP) PROVIDES: 1 PROTEIN; 2 VEGETABLES; ½ BREAD; 10 OPTIONAL CALORIES.
PER SERVING: 127 CALORIES; 11 G PROTEIN; 1 G FAT; 19 G CARBOHYDRATE; 376 MG SODIUM;
19 MG CHOLESTEROL; 2 G DIETARY FIBER.

REDUCED FAT AND CHOLESTEROL

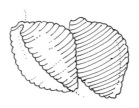

Vegetable Fettuccine

Makes 4 servings

Colorful strips of carrot, squash and bell pepper make up this simple primavera. Try it with a spinach or herb-flavored fettuccine if available.

1 packet instant chicken broth mix
2 medium carrots, cut into strips
1 medium red or green bell pepper, cut into strips
1 medium zucchini or yellow squash, cut into strips

4½ ounces fettuccine, cooked and drained
2 tablespoons + 2 teaspoons reduced-calorie tub margarine
1 tablespoon minced scallion
Freshly ground black pepper to taste

1. In an 11x7" baking dish, dissolve broth mix in ¼ cup water. Add carrots; microwave, covered, on High 3-4 minutes, until softened.

2. Add bell pepper and zucchini; microwave, covered, on High 3-4 minutes, until vegetables are tender-crisp, stirring halfway through cooking. Stir in fettuccine and margarine; toss gently to combine. Sprinkle with scallion and freshly ground black pepper to taste.

EACH SERVING PROVIDES: 1 FAT; 2 VEGETABLES; 1¹/2 BREADS; 3 OPTIONAL CALORIES.
PER SERVING: 190 CALORIES; 6 G PROTEIN; 5 G FAT; 31 G CARBOHYDRATE; 365 MG SODIUM;
30 MG CHOLESTEROL; 3 G DIETARY FIBER.

REDUCED FAT

Pasta with Spring Vegetables

Makes 4 servings

Fresh vegetables get a tangy taste from mustard and lemon juice. Serve this dish with grilled chicken breasts for a carefree summer meal.

2 medium carrots, halved lengthwise and cut into 2" pieces
¼ cup reduced-sodium chicken broth
18 medium asparagus spears, cut into 2" pieces
½ cup sliced radishes
1 tablespoon + 1 teaspoon reduced-calorie tub margarine

2 teaspoons lemon juice
1 teaspoon Dijon-style mustard
4½ ounces wide noodles, cooked and drained
1 tablespoon minced scallion
½ teaspoon dried tarragon or savory

1. In an 11x7" baking dish, combine carrots and chicken broth. Microwave, covered, on High 4 minutes. Arrange asparagus and radishes at edges of dish; microwave, covered, 2-4 minutes, until vegetables are tender-crisp.

2. Stir in margarine, lemon juice and mustard. Add noodles; toss gently to combine. Sprinkle with scallion and tarragon.

EACH SERVING PROVIDES: ¹/₂ FAT; 2 VEGETABLES; 1¹/₂ BREADS; 3 OPTIONAL CALORIES.
PER SERVING: 173 CALORIES; 6 G PROTEIN; 4 G FAT; 30 G CARBOHYDRATE; 143 MG SODIUM; 30 MG CHOLESTEROL; 3 G DIETARY FIBER.

REDUCED FAT AND SODIUM

MICROWAVE
Slim Ways with Pasta

Pasta Florentine

137

Makes 4 servings

Five ingredients combine to make this basic dish. In the microwave, cooked spaghetti is warmed while the mozzarella melts.

2 cups frozen leaf spinach
  (one 10-ounce package)
4-6 garlic cloves, finely chopped
6 ounces thin spaghetti, cooked
  and drained

6 ounces shredded part-skim
  mozzarella cheese
1 tablespoon + 1 teaspoon grated
  Parmesan cheese

1. Spray a 2-quart casserole with nonstick cooking spray. Place frozen spinach in casserole; microwave, covered, on High 5 minutes. Stir and add garlic; microwave, covered, on High 2 minutes.

2. Add remaining ingredients to casserole; stir to combine. Microwave, covered, on High 2 minutes, until heated through.

EACH SERVING PROVIDES: 2 PROTEINS; 1 VEGETABLE; 2 BREADS; 10 OPTIONAL CALORIES.
PER SERVING: 417 CALORIES; 31 G PROTEIN; 15 G FAT; 43 G CARBOHYDRATE; 584 MG SODIUM;
45 MG CHOLESTEROL; 6 G DIETARY FIBER.

REDUCED CHOLESTEROL

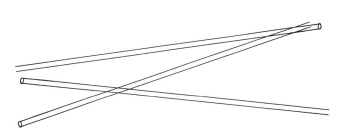

138 Rigatoni with Garden Vegetables

Makes 4 servings

Chunks of vegetables and whole mushroooms are tossed with rigatoni and topped with mozzarella cheese.

2 medium red or yellow onions, halved and sliced
2 medium yellow, green or red bell peppers, sliced
1 medium zucchini or yellow squash, halved and sliced
4½ ounces rigatoni, cooked and drained

2 cups sliced mushrooms
1 packet instant chicken broth mix
½ teaspoon paprika
1½ ounces shredded part-skim mozzarella cheese

1. In an 11x7" baking dish, combine onions, peppers, zucchini and 2 tablespoons water. Microwave, covered, on High 4-5 minutes, stirring vegetables halfway through cooking.

2. Add rigatoni and mushrooms to dish; toss to combine with vegetables. Sprinkle with broth mix and paprika. Microwave, covered, on High 2-3 minutes, until vegetables are tender. Sprinkle with mozzarella cheese; microwave, uncovered, on High 2-3 minutes, until cheese melts.

EACH SERVING PROVIDES: ½ PROTEIN; 3 VEGETABLES; 1½ BREADS; 3 OPTIONAL CALORIES.
PER SERVING: 191 CALORIES; 9 G PROTEIN; 3 G FAT; 34 G CARBOHYDRATE; 307 MG SODIUM;
6 MG CHOLESTEROL; 2 G DIETARY FIBER.

REDUCED CHOLESTEROL AND FAT

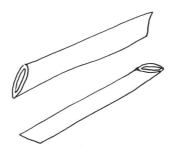

139 Pasta with Peppers and Onions

Makes 4 servings

In less than nine minutes, this tasty, inexpensive dish is ready to serve. Basic ingredients make it easy to prepare this flavor-packed pasta any time.

3 medium green, red or yellow bell peppers, cut into strips
2 cups thinly sliced onions
1/4 teaspoon dried oregano
1/4 teaspoon salt
1/8 teaspoon freshly ground black pepper

1 1/2 ounces shredded part-skim mozzarella cheese
2 tablespoons grated Parmesan cheese
6 ounces spaghetti, cooked and drained

1. In a 2 1/2-quart casserole, combine peppers, onions, oregano, salt and pepper; microwave, covered, on High 6-7 minutes, until tender-crisp, stirring halfway through cooking.

2. Add mozzarella and Parmesan cheese; toss to combine. Let stand, covered, 1-2 minutes, until cheese melts. Add spaghetti; toss to combine.

EACH SERVING PROVIDES: 1/2 PROTEIN; 2 1/2 VEGETABLES; 2 BREADS; 15 OPTIONAL CALORIES.
PER SERVING: 246 CALORIES; 11 G PROTEIN; 3 G FAT; 44 G CARBOHYDRATE; 238 MG SODIUM;
8 MG CHOLESTEROL; 3 G DIETARY FIBER.

REDUCED FAT AND CHOLESTEROL

Pasta with Spinach, Bacon and Mushrooms

Makes 4 servings

Pappardelle noodles would be a fine alternate choice in this dish, which combines three great tastes. You can also try this pasta with turkey bacon.

6 cups spinach leaves
2 slices bacon
1 ½ cups sliced mushrooms
½ cup chopped onion
4 ½ ounces wide noodles, cooked
   and drained

2 tablespoons cider vinegar
2 teaspoons vegetable oil
1 tablespoon Dijon mustard
¼ teaspoon cracked black pepper

1. Thoroughly wash spinach; drain and cut into bite-sized pieces. Set aside.

2. In a 2½-quart casserole, microwave bacon on High 3-4 minutes, until crisp; remove to paper towel to drain; crumble. Wipe out casserole; add mushrooms and onion. Microwave, covered, on High 1-2 minutes, until softened. Add spinach; microwave, covered, 45 seconds-1½ minutes, until spinach wilts.

3. Add noodles, vinegar, oil, mustard and pepper to casserole; toss gently to combine. Sprinkle with bacon.

EACH SERVING PROVIDES: ½ FAT; 4 VEGETABLES; 1½ BREADS; 20 OPTIONAL CALORIES.
PER SERVING: 198 CALORIES; 9 G PROTEIN; 6 G FAT; 30 G CARBOHYDRATE; 238 MG SODIUM;
33 MG CHOLESTEROL; 4 G DIETARY FIBER.

REDUCED FAT

Spicy Pasta with Broccoli

Makes 4 servings

Broccoli and garlic are a match made in heaven—Italian heaven! Roasted red pepper adds color to this dish, which is delicious served hot or cold.

1 tablespoon + 1 teaspoon olive oil
2 garlic cloves, minced
2 cups drained thawed frozen cut broccoli (one 10-ounce package)
½ cup drained roasted red pepper, coarsely chopped

1 tablespoon lemon juice
¼ teaspoon salt
⅛ teaspoon crushed red pepper flakes
4½ ounces rigatoni, cooked and drained

1. In a 2-quart casserole, combine oil and garlic. Microwave, covered, on High 1 minute, until softened.

2. Add broccoli, roasted red pepper, lemon juice, salt and red pepper flakes. Microwave, covered, on High 2-3 minutes, until hot. Add rigatoni; toss to combine.

EACH SERVING PROVIDES: 1 FAT; 1¼ VEGETABLES; 1½ BREADS.
PER SERVING: 185 CALORIES; 6 G PROTEIN; 5 G FAT; 29 G CARBOHYDRATE; 159 MG SODIUM;
0 MG CHOLESTEROL; 2 G DIETARY FIBER.

REDUCED FAT AND SODIUM; CHOLESTEROL-FREE

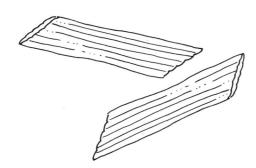

MICROWAVE
Slim Ways with Pasta

Pasta with Tomatoes and Shrimp

Makes 4 servings

Mushrooms, garlic and white wine add depth of flavor to shrimp. To speed preparation, have the fish market peel and devein the shrimp for you.

1 tablespoon + 1 teaspoon olive oil
2 garlic cloves, minced
2 cups coarsely chopped tomatoes
8 medium mushrooms, thickly sliced
10 ounces shelled deveined shrimp
2 tablespoons finely chopped fresh
   dill, or 1 teaspoon dried

1 tablespoon lemon juice
1 tablespoon dry white wine
4½ ounces medium pasta shells,
   cooked and drained

1. In a 2½-quart casserole, microwave oil and garlic on High 1 minute, until softened. Add tomatoes and mushrooms; microwave, covered, 4-5 minutes, stirring halfway through cooking.

2. Add shrimp, arranging with tails toward center of casserole. Sprinkle with dill, lemon juice and wine. Microwave, covered, on High 2½-4 minutes, just until shrimp turn pink, rearranging shrimp and stirring halfway through cooking.

3. Stir pasta into casserole; toss to combine.

EACH SERVING PROVIDES: 1 FAT; 1 PROTEIN; 1½ VEGETABLES; 1½ BREADS; 3 OPTIONAL CALORIES.
PER SERVING: 265 CALORIES; 20 G PROTEIN; 7 G FAT; 31 G CARBOHYDRATE; 118 MG SODIUM;
108 MG CHOLESTEROL; 2 G DIETARY FIBER.

REDUCED FAT AND SODIUM

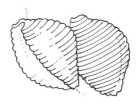

143 Chicken Chinoise with Angel Hair

Makes 4 servings

This chicken dish is like making a stir-fry in your microwave! It's also good over cellophane noodles.

10 ounces boneless skinless chicken breasts, partially frozen
3 tablespoons reduced-sodium soy sauce
1 tablespoon + 1 teaspoon vegetable oil
1 teaspoon cornstarch
½ teaspoon sugar
½ teaspoon ground ginger

1 medium carrot, diagonally sliced
½ cup diagonally sliced bok choy (Chinese cabbage) or celery
1 garlic clove, minced
4 scallions, cut into 2" pieces
¼ cup thinly sliced bell pepper
4½ ounces angel hair pasta, cooked and drained

1. Cut chicken crosswise into very thin slices; set aside.

2. In a 2½-quart casserole, combine soy sauce, oil, cornstarch, sugar, ginger and 2 tablespoons water. Add carrot, bok choy and garlic; microwave, covered, on High 1-2 minutes.

3. Add chicken and scallions; microwave, covered, on High 2-3 minutes, until chicken is no longer pink. Sprinkle with bell pepper; let stand, covered, 1 minute to wilt pepper. Add pasta; toss to combine.

EACH SERVING PROVIDES: 1 FAT; 2 PROTEINS; 1 VEGETABLE; 1½ BREADS; 5 OPTIONAL CALORIES.
PER SERVING: 266 CALORIES; 22 G PROTEIN; 6 G FAT; 30 G CARBOHYDRATE; 514 MG SODIUM;
41 MG CHOLESTEROL; 2 G DIETARY FIBER.

REDUCED FAT AND CHOLESTEROL

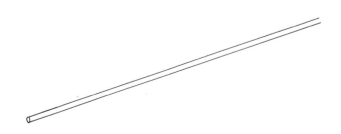

Curried Chicken with Couscous

Makes 4 servings

This Moroccan pasta is naturally quick-cooking. Its hearty taste and sturdy texture are a match for curried vegetables and chicken.

1½ pounds chicken thighs
1 medium zucchini or yellow squash, halved and sliced
1 cup chopped onion
1 tablespoon + 1 teaspoon vegetable oil
1 garlic clove, minced

1 tablespoon curry powder
1 tablespoon all-purpose flour
2 cups canned tomatoes
¼ cup seedless raisins
4 ounces couscous, cooked and fluffed with fork

1. Remove skin and trim all visible fat from chicken thighs; set chicken aside.

2. In a 2½-quart casserole, combine zucchini, onion, oil and garlic; microwave, covered, on High 2-3 minutes. Stir in curry powder and flour until blended. Add tomatoes with their liquid, breaking up tomatoes with spoon, and raisins.

3. Add chicken thighs, arranging meatier portions toward outer edges of casserole. Microwave, covered, 16-18 minutes, until chicken and zucchini are tender, rearranging chicken and stirring halfway through cooking.

4. To serve, spoon couscous into shallow serving bowl; top with chicken mixture.

EACH SERVING PROVIDES: 1 FAT; 2 PROTEINS; 2 VEGETABLES; 1 BREAD; ½ FRUIT; 10 OPTIONAL CALORIES.
PER SERVING: 351 CALORIES; 21 G PROTEIN; 12 G FAT; 42 G CARBOHYDRATE; 253 MG SODIUM;
54 MG CHOLESTEROL; 3 G DIETARY FIBER.

REDUCED FAT AND SODIUM

145 Pork with Apples and Noodles

Makes 4 servings

A perfect autumn dish. Paprika and parsley give color to this pork mixture, served on hot noodles.

10 ounces boneless pork tenderloin, cut into thin 2" strips
2 teaspoons olive oil
1 cup chopped onion
2 garlic cloves, minced
½ teaspoon paprika
½ cup low-sodium beef broth
1 teaspoon cornstarch

2 small Granny Smith apples, cored and coarsely chopped
¼ teaspoon salt
Pinch ground red pepper
1 medium tomato, cut into ½" wedges
6 ounces wide noodles, cooked and drained
Parsley to garnish

1. Place pork strips on rack over tray. Microwave on High 1 minute; set aside.

2. Place oil in a 2-quart casserole; microwave on High 1 minute. Add pork, onion, garlic and paprika; cover and microwave on Medium 5 minutes, stirring twice.

3. In a 1-cup measure, stir broth and cornstarch until dissolved. Add to casserole with apples, salt and red pepper. Cover and microwave on High 4 minutes; stir and add tomato. Cover and microwave on High 3 minutes longer, until apples are tender. Let stand, covered, 5 minutes.

4. To serve, place noodles on serving plate. Top with pork mixture; toss to combine. Garnish with parsley.

EACH SERVING PROVIDES: ¹/₂ FAT; 2 PROTEINS; 1 VEGETABLE; 2 BREADS; ¹/₂ FRUIT; 10 OPTIONAL CALORIES.
PER SERVING: 389 CALORIES; 25 G PROTEIN; 8 G FAT; 55 G CARBOHYDRATE; 190 MG SODIUM;
106 MG CHOLESTEROL; 6 G DIETARY FIBER.

REDUCED FAT AND SODIUM

Pork and Rotini Casserole

Makes 4 servings

This hearty casserole combines a lean cut of pork with red bell pepper, spicy scallions and pasta spirals.

10 ounces boneless lean pork,
   cut into ½" cubes
½ cup sliced scallions
3 ounces tri-color rotini pasta
1 tablespoon + 1 teaspoon olive oil
1 cup low-sodium chicken broth

½ cup sliced red bell pepper
½ cup sliced green bell pepper
½ cup diced tomato
½ teaspoon dried oregano

1. Place pork cubes on rack over tray. Microwave on High 1 minute; set aside.

2. In a 2-quart casserole, combine scallions, pasta and oil; stir to coat pasta. Microwave, covered, on High 4 minutes, stirring once.

3. Stir in pork and remaining ingredients. Microwave, covered, on High 5 minutes; stir. Microwave, covered, on Medium 20-23 minutes, or until pasta is tender, stirring every 5 minutes. Let stand 4 minutes.

EACH SERVING PROVIDES: 1 FAT; 2 PROTEINS; 1 VEGETABLE; 1 BREAD; 10 OPTIONAL CALORIES.
PER SERVING: 270 CALORIES; 19 G PROTEIN; 13 G FAT; 19 G CARBOHYDRATE; 66 MG SODIUM;
53 MG CHOLESTEROL; 2 G DIETARY FIBER.

REDUCED SODIUM

Fusilli with Red Clam Sauce

147

Makes 4 servings

This classic sauce is a quick fix when prepared in the microwave. The corkscrew-shaped pasta will catch and hold the chunky sauce.

1½ cups chopped drained canned
   tomatoes
8 ounces drained canned whole clams
   (reserve ¼ cup liquid)
1 cup sliced green bell pepper
½ cup diced onion
¼ cup chopped fresh flat-leaf parsley

1 garlic clove, minced
½ teaspoon dried basil
¼ teaspoon dried oregano
3 ounces fusilli, cooked and drained
1 tablespoon grated Parmesan cheese

1. In a 2-quart casserole, combine tomatoes, clams and reserved liquid, bell pepper, onion, parsley, garlic, basil and oregano. Microwave, covered, on High 4½ minutes, stirring twice.

2. Place pasta in large serving bowl; spoon sauce over pasta. Sprinkle with Parmesan cheese; toss to combine.

EACH SERVING PROVIDES: 1 PROTEIN; 1½ VEGETABLES; 1 BREAD; 10 OPTIONAL CALORIES.
PER SERVING: 204 CALORIES; 19 G PROTEIN; 2 G FAT; 27 G CARBOHYDRATE; 270 MG SODIUM;
39 MG CHOLESTEROL; 2 G DIETARY FIBER.

REDUCED FAT

Spaghetti with Meat Sauce

Makes 4 servings

Unlike traditional meat sauce, which can be an all-day affair, you can whip up this sauce, using ground beef or turkey, in less than 20 minutes—plenty of time to cook the spaghetti and toss together a crunchy salad.

1 tablespoon + 1 teaspoon olive oil
½ cup chopped onion
2 garlic cloves, minced
10 ounces ground turkey
2 cups thickly sliced mushrooms
½ teaspoon dried oregano

½ teaspoon salt
2 cups canned tomatoes
¼ cup tomato paste
6 ounces spaghetti, cooked
  and drained

1. In a 2½-quart casserole, combine oil, onion and garlic; microwave, covered, on High 2-3 minutes, until softened.

2. Add turkey, mushrooms, oregano and salt. Microwave, covered, on High 4-5 minutes, until turkey is no longer pink, stirring halfway through cooking.

3. Add tomatoes with their liquid, breaking up tomatoes with spoon, and tomato paste. Microwave, covered, on High 8-10 minutes, stirring halfway through cooking.

4. Add spaghetti to casserole; toss to combine with sauce.

EACH SERVING PROVIDES: 1 FAT; 2 PROTEINS; 2½ VEGETABLES; 2 BREADS.
PER SERVING: 355 CALORIES; 21 G PROTEIN; 11 G FAT; 44 G CARBOHYDRATE; 670 MG SODIUM;
52 MG CHOLESTEROL; 3 G DIETARY FIBER.

REDUCED FAT

Turkey Lasagna Rolls

Makes 6 servings

A new take—individual rolls mean less preparation time, and they're perfect to satisfy a summer craving for lasagna without oven heat.

2 cups low-sodium tomato sauce
2 tablespoons chopped fresh basil
¼ teaspoon dried oregano
¼ teaspoon salt
1½ cups sliced fresh mushrooms
1 cup chopped zucchini
½ cup chopped onion
2 tablespoons reduced-calorie
   tub margarine
1 cup part-skim ricotta cheese

2 ounces cooked turkey breast,
   shredded
2 teaspoons grated Parmesan cheese
Pinch ground nutmeg
18 whole basil leaves
4½ ounces lasagna noodles (about
   6), cooked and drained
3 ounces shredded part-skim
   mozzarella cheese

1. In a 1-quart measure, combine tomato sauce, chopped basil, oregano and salt. Microwave on High 2 minutes, stirring after 1 minute.

2. In large bowl, combine mushrooms, zucchini, onion and margarine. Microwave on High 3-4 minutes, stirring after 2 minutes, until tender; set aside.

3. Add ricotta, turkey, Parmesan cheese and nutmeg to the vegetables; stir to mix well.

4. In a 13x9" baking dish, spread ¾ cup tomato sauce; set aside.

5. Spread out lasagna noodles on work surface. With small spatula, spread 1 tablespoon tomato sauce over each noodle. Spread each evenly with ½ cup ricotta mixture and 3 basil leaves. Roll noodles from short end to enclose filling.

6. Place lasagna rolls seam-side down in prepared dish. Top evenly with remaining tomato sauce; sprinkle evenly with mozzarella.

7. Microwave on High 5-7 minutes, turning dish once, until sauce is bubbly.

EACH SERVING PROVIDES: ½ FAT; 2 PROTEINS; 1²/₃ VEGETABLES; 1 BREAD;
2 OPTIONAL CALOIRES.
PER SERVING: 245 CALORIES; 16 G PROTEIN; 8 G FAT; 27 G CARBOHYDRATE; 288 MG SODIUM; 29 MG
CHOLESTEROL; 2 G DIETARY FIBER.

REDUCED FAT

150 Lasagna with Fresh Tomato Sauce

Makes 6 servings

Save time with a new convenience product, no-boil lasagna noodles that do not have to be pre-cooked. If you are using regular lasagna noodles, prepare them following label directions.

½ cup chopped onion
1 tablespoon olive oil
2 garlic cloves, minced
4 cups coarsely chopped tomatoes
½ cup meatless spaghetti sauce
¼ cup tomato sauce
1 teaspoon dried basil

1¾ cups part-skim ricotta cheese
1 egg
¼ teaspoon freshly ground black pepper
9 ounces no-boil or regular lasagna noodles (about 9 noodles)
3 ounces shredded part-skim

1. To prepare sauce, in a 2-quart casserole, combine onion, oil and garlic. Microwave, covered, on High 2-3 minutes, until softened. Add tomatoes, spaghetti sauce, tomato sauce and basil; microwave, covered, 4-5 minutes, until tomatoes are soft, but still hold their shape. Set aside.

2. In medium bowl, combine ricotta cheese, egg and pepper. To assemble lasagna, spread ½ cup of the tomato mixture in an 11x7" baking dish. Top with 3 lasagna noodles, one-third of the tomato mixture, half the ricotta mixture and one-third of the mozzarella cheese. Repeat layering. Arrange remaining 3 noodles on top; top with remaining tomato mixture and mozzarella cheese.

3. Cover baking dish with vented plastic wrap; place dish on microwave cooking rack (or inverted pie plate). Microwave on High 8-10 minutes, until hot and bubbly, rotating dish halfway through cooking. Let stand 5 minutes before cutting.

EACH SERVING PROVIDES: ½ FAT; 2 PROTEINS; 2 VEGETABLES; 2 BREADS; 5 OPTIONAL CALORIES.
PER SERVING: 379 CALORIES; 20 G PROTEIN; 12 G FAT; 45 G CARBOHYDRATE; 344 MG SODIUM;
66 MG CHOLESTEROL; 2 G DIETARY FIBER.

151 Deli Pasta Salad

Makes 6 servings

Bits of cheddar cheese and beef salami flavor this crunchy pasta salad. You can substitute Swiss or Jarlsberg cheese and ham or prosciutto for a different taste.

4½ ounces bow tie pasta, cooked and drained
4 cups cauliflower florets
1 cup sliced carrots
12 cherry tomatoes, halved
5 pitted small ripe olives, halved

3 tablespoons reduced-calorie Italian dressing (6 calories per tablespoon)
1½ ounces reduced-fat cheddar cheese, diced
1 ounce beef salami, chopped

1. Place bow ties in serving bowl; refrigerate while preparing vegetables.

2. In a 2½-quart casserole, microwave cauliflower with ¼ cup water, covered, on High 6-8 minutes, until tender-crisp, stirring halfway through cooking. Rinse under cold water to chill; drain and add to bowl with bow ties.

3. In same casserole, microwave carrots with 2 tablespoons water, covered, on High 2-3 minutes, until tender-crisp, stirring halfway through cooking. Rinse under cold water to chill; drain. Add carrots, cherry tomatoes and olives to bowl. Toss with salad dressing; sprinkle with cheese and salami.

EACH SERVING PROVIDES: ½ PROTEIN; 2 VEGETABLES; 1 BREAD; 15 OPTIONAL CALORIES.
PER SERVING: 154 CALORIES; 7 G PROTEIN; 4 G FAT; 23 G CARBOHYDRATE; 279 MG SODIUM;
10 MG CHOLESTEROL; 3 G DIETARY FIBER.

REDUCED FAT AND CHOLESTEROL

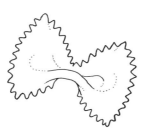

Macaroni and Vegetable Slaw

Makes 4 servings

Try this instead of cole slaw at your next picnic—it can be served hot or cold and uses prepared salad dressing for a quick fix.

1 ½ cups coarsely chopped red or
   green cabbage
½ cup thinly sliced carrot
½ cup finely chopped onion
½ cup chopped yellow squash
3 ounces elbow macaroni, cooked,
   drained and rinsed

¼ cup reduced-calorie Italian
   dressing (6 calories per tablespoon)
Salt and freshly ground black pepper
   to taste

1. In a 2-quart casserole, combine cabbage, carrot, onion, squash and 2 tablespoons water; microwave, covered, on High 2 minutes. Let stand, covered, 1-2 minutes, until vegetables are slightly wilted. Rinse under cold water to chill; drain.

2. Place macaroni in large bowl; add vegetables, dressing, salt and pepper to taste; toss to combine. Cover and refrigerate at least 1 hour to blend flavors.

EACH SERVING PROVIDES: 1¹/₂ VEGETABLES; 1 BREAD; 6 OPTIONAL CALORIES.
PER SERVING: 109 CALORIES; 4 G PROTEIN; 0 G FAT; 23 G CARBOHYDRATE; 220 MG SODIUM;
0 MG CHOLESTEROL; 2 G DIETARY FIBER.

REDUCED FAT; CHOLESTEROL-FREE

MICROWAVE
Slim Ways with Pasta

Orzo Pilaf

Makes 4 servings

This risotto-inspired pilaf, dotted with scallion and peas, is a perfect side dish for beef or poultry and is easy to prepare. For even more flavor, add a little finely chopped prosciutto just before serving.

1 cup reduced-sodium chicken broth
3 ounces orzo
1 cup thawed frozen peas
2 tablespoons minced scallion
2 tablespoons grated Parmesan cheese

1 tablespoon + 1 teaspoon reduced-calorie tub margarine
⅛ teaspoon freshly ground black pepper

1. In a 2½-quart casserole, combine chicken broth, orzo and 1 cup water. Microwave, covered, on High 6-7 minutes (mixture will come to a boil). Reduce power to Medium-High; stir; cook 2 minutes; stir again. Cook 3-4 minutes longer, until orzo is almost tender; stir.

2. Add peas, scallion, Parmesan cheese, margarine and pepper. Let stand, covered, 5-6 minutes, until liquid is absorbed and orzo is tender.

Variation: Stir in 2 ounces minced prosciutto just before serving. (Add ½ Protein per serving.)

EACH SERVING PROVIDES: ½ FAT; 1¼ BREADS; 25 OPTIONAL CALORIES.
PER SERVING: 141 CALORIES; 6 G PROTEIN; 3 G FAT; 21 G CARBOHYDRATE; 285 MG SODIUM;
2 MG CHOLESTEROL; 2 G DIETARY FIBER.

REDUCED CHOLESTEROL AND FAT

Salads

Pasta salads have come a long way from the much-maligned, mayo-laden macaroni salad of yesteryear. Today's salad bars are filled with every conceivable pasta-vegetable-meat-cheese combination. What makes a chilled pasta salad different than a traditional heated dish are lighter dressings and sauces. These salads usually require some standing time to absorb the flavors of a dressing, giving the pasta an almost marinated taste. Some should be served from the refrigerator; others taste their best at room temperature. The addition of crunchy vegetables make these dishes not only tasty but nutritious, and for many, the only cooking necessary is boiling the pasta, which makes these salads ideal for speedy summer meals. Enjoy ethnic-inspired salads such as Cellophane Noodles and Seafood or Whole-Wheat Oriental Spaghetti Salad, or the basics—Pasta with Spring Vegetables or Antipasto Salad, featuring cheese tortellini and some of your favorites from the deli. Mexican Salsa Salad combines the tastes of chili and nachos for a spicy blend that's sure to be a hit. Three cheeses are tossed with ziti to make Ricotta Salad, served with a sauce of fresh tomato, basil and garlic. An added attraction of these quick-fix dishes is that many use basic ingredients you may already have in your refrigerator and pantry.

Roasted Vegetable-Pasta Salad

155

Makes 4 servings

The intense flavor of these roasted vegetables comes alive when chilled. Serve with slices of fresh mozzarella and a scattering of shredded fresh basil.

2 tablespoons Dijon mustard
1 tablespoon + 1 teaspoon olive oil
1 tablespoon lemon juice
2 garlic cloves, minced
¼ teaspoon salt
⅛ teaspoon freshly ground black pepper
1 medium red bell pepper, cut into strips

1 medium green bell pepper, cut into strips
1 medium yellow bell pepper, cut into strips
1 cup cubed eggplant, cut into ½" pieces
4½ ounces rotelle, cooked, drained and rinsed

1. Preheat oven to 350°F. In small bowl, combine mustard, oil, lemon juice, garlic, salt and black pepper.

2. In a 13x9" baking pan, combine bell peppers and eggplant; toss with mustard mixture. Roast 20-25 minutes, until vegetables are tender; set aside; let cool.

3. Place pasta in large serving bowl; add vegetables. Toss to combine; cover and refrigerate until well chilled. Stir salad before serving.

EACH SERVING (1 CUP) PROVIDES: 1 FAT; 2 VEGETABLES; 1½ BREADS.
PER SERVING: 195 CALORIES; 5 G PROTEIN; 6 G FAT; 31 G CARBOHYDRATE; 366 MG SODIUM;
0 MG CHOLESTEROL; 2 G DIETARY FIBER.

REDUCED FAT; CHOLESTEROL-FREE

SALADS
Slim Ways with Pasta

Linguine-Vegetable Salad

Makes 4 servings

The fresh crunch of snow peas and zucchini gets a kick from the sizzle of a garlicky, spicy red pepper sauce, and lots of scallions.

6 ounces linguine, cooked, drained and rinsed
1 pound drained cooked chick-peas
2 cups julienned snow peas
2 cups thinly sliced zucchini
12 cherry tomatoes, halved
1 cup chopped scallions

¼ cup tomato puree
¼ cup fresh lime juice
2 garlic cloves, halved
1 tablespoon red wine vinegar
2 teaspoons olive oil
2 drops hot red pepper sauce, or to taste

1. In large bowl, combine linguine, chick-peas, snow peas, zucchini and tomatoes; set aside.

2. To prepare dressing, in mini food processor, combine remaining ingredients and 1 tablespoon water; process until smooth. Pour dressing over linguine mixture; toss to coat well.

EACH SERVING PROVIDES: ¹/₂ FAT; 2 PROTEINS; 3¹/₄ VEGETABLES; 2 BREADS.
PER SERVING: 431 CALORIES; 19 G PROTEIN; 6 G FAT; 77 G CARBOHYDRATE; 86 MG SODIUM;
0 MG CHOLESTEROL; 9 G DIETARY FIBER.

REDUCED FAT AND SODIUM; CHOLESTEROL-FREE

157 Broccoli and Whole-Wheat Pasta Salad

Makes 4 servings

Chick-peas add protein to this hearty salad that boasts 6 grams of dietary fiber.

4½ ounces whole-wheat spaghetti
2 cups broccoli florets
1 cup chopped tomatoes
1 tablespoon + 1 teaspoon olive oil
1 tablespoon red wine vinegar

1 teaspoon low-sodium soy sauce
Pinch ground white pepper
8 ounces drained cooked chick-peas
2 tablespoons grated Parmesan
  cheese

1. In large pot of boiling water, cook spaghetti 5 minutes. Add broccoli; cook 5-8 minutes longer, until spaghetti and broccoli are tender. Drain and place in large serving bowl.

2. To prepare dressing, in small bowl, combine tomatoes, oil, vinegar, soy sauce and pepper.

3. Pour dressing over spaghetti; toss to mix well. Add chick-peas and cheese; mix well. Cover and refrigerate at least 1 hour, until well chilled.

EACH SERVING PROVIDES: 1 FAT; 1 PROTEIN; 1¹/₂ VEGETABLES; 1¹/₂ BREADS; 15 OPTIONAL CALORIES.
PER SERVING: 285 CALORIES; 13 G PROTEIN; 7 G FAT; 46 G CARBOHYDRATE; 105 MG SODIUM;
2 MG CHOLESTEROL; 6 G DIETARY FIBER.

REDUCED FAT, SODIUM AND CHOLESTEROL

158 Antipasto Salad

Makes 4 servings

A wonderful pasta course for a special meal, or to tote for a picnic lunch. The use of mostly prepared ingredients gives new meaning to the words quick fix!

2 tablespoons white wine vinegar
1 tablespoon + 1 teaspoon olive oil
1 tablespoon minced shallots
1 teaspoon dried oregano
⅛ teaspoon dried red pepper flakes

2 cups cooked cheese tortellini, cooled
1 medium red bell pepper, cut
   into thin strips
3 ounces provolone cheese, cubed
2 ounces beef salami, cut into strips

1. To prepare dressing, in small bowl, combine vinegar, oil, shallots, oregano and red pepper flakes.

2. In medium bowl, combine tortellini, bell pepper, cheese and salami. Add dressing; toss to coat.

EACH SERVING (1 CUP) PROVIDES: 1 FAT; 2½ PROTEINS; ½ VEGETABLE; 1 BREAD; 20 OPTIONAL CALORIES.
PER SERVING: 336 CALORIES; 17 G PROTEIN; 16 G FAT; 31 G CARBOHYDRATE; 615 MG SODIUM; 56 MG CHOLESTEROL; 0 G DIETARY FIBER.

Ziti and Cheese Salad

Makes 4 servings

This tangy dressing, low in fat and cholesterol, tastes rich and creamy. At just 45 calories for a 3-tablespoon serving, you'll want to try it on other salads too.

6 tablespoons plain nonfat yogurt
2 tablespoons + 2 teaspoons reduced-calorie mayonnaise
2 tablespoons chopped fresh dill
2 teaspoons sweet pickle relish
1 teaspoon drained white horseradish
½ teaspoon paprika

4½ ounces ziti, cooked, drained and rinsed
4 ounces reduced-calorie cheddar cheese, cubed
2 cups blanched trimmed green beans
12 cherry tomatoes, halved
Romaine lettuce leaves

1. To prepare dressing, in small bowl, combine yogurt, mayonnaise, dill, relish, horseradish and paprika; set aside.

2. In large bowl, combine ziti, cheese, beans and tomatoes. Add dressing; toss to mix well. Cover and refrigerate at least 1 hour, until well chilled. Serve on lettuce leaves.

EACH SERVING PROVIDES: 1 FAT; 1 PROTEIN; 1½ VEGETABLES; 1½ BREADS; 15 OPTIONAL CALORIES.
PER SERVING: 276 CALORIES; 15 G PROTEIN; 8 G FAT; 34 G CARBOHYDRATE; 299 MG SODIUM;
24 MG CHOLESTEROL; 2 G DIETARY FIBER.

REDUCED FAT AND CHOLESTEROL

160 Ricotta Pasta Salad

Makes 4 servings

Three cheeses, tomatoes, basil and plenty of garlic unite for a chilled version of baked ziti. Make this when summer provides an abundance of sun-ripened tomatoes and fragrant fresh herbs.

4 medium tomatoes, seeded and diced
¼ cup chopped fresh basil
4 garlic cloves, minced
4½ ounces ziti, cooked, drained and rinsed
1 tablespoon + 1 teaspoon olive oil
1 cup part-skim ricotta cheese

3 ounces shredded part-skim mozzarella cheese
2 tablespoons grated Parmesan cheese
¼ teaspoon nutmeg
¼ teaspoon freshly ground black pepper

1. In medium bowl, combine tomatoes, basil and garlic; toss to mix well. Cover and refrigerate at least 2 hours, stirring occasionally.

2. In large serving bowl, combine ziti and oil; toss to coat. Stir in tomato mixture. Add ricotta, mozzarella, Parmesan, nutmeg and pepper; toss to combine. Cover and refrigerate at least 1 hour, until well chilled.

EACH SERVING PROVIDES: 1 FAT; 2 PROTEINS; 2 VEGETABLES; 1½ BREADS; 15 OPTIONAL CALORIES.
PER SERVING: 349 CALORIES; 19 G PROTEIN; 15 G FAT; 37 G CARBOHYDRATE; 240 MG SODIUM;
33 MG CHOLESTEROL; 3 G DIETARY FIBER.

REDUCED SODIUM AND CHOLESTEROL

Feta and Olive Pasta Salad

161

Makes 4 servings

Serve this Greek-inspired salad with diced red and yellow bell pepper with grilled lamb or bluefish; the next day it will make a colorful take-along lunch.

3 ounces crumbled feta cheese
10 small Calamata olives, pitted and
  chopped
¼ cup coarsely chopped fresh basil
1 tablespoon olive oil

¼ teaspoon dried red pepper flakes
4½ ounces medium pasta shells,
  cooked, drained and rinsed
½ medium red bell pepper, diced
½ medium yellow bell pepper, diced

1. In large serving bowl, combine feta cheese, olives, basil, olive oil and pepper flakes; set aside for 30 minutes.

2. Add pasta shells and red and yellow peppers to serving bowl; toss to mix well. Cover and refrigerate at least 1 hour, until well chilled. Toss well before serving.

EACH SERVING PROVIDES: 1 FAT; 1 PROTEIN; 1/2 VEGETABLE; 11/2 BREADS.

PER SERVING: 238 CALORIES; 8 G PROTEIN; 11 G FAT; 28 G CARBOHYDRATE; 473 MG SODIUM;

19 MG CHOLESTEROL; 1 G DIETARY FIBER.

REDUCED CHOLESTEROL

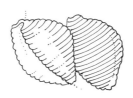

Whole-Wheat Fettuccine with Shrimp

162

Makes 4 servings

Line plates with colorful lettuce leaves and pile on this bright mix of pasta, shrimp and crisp vegetables in a tangy mustard-tarragon dressing. Serve with white wine and fresh strawberries for a perfect summer meal.

6 ounces whole-wheat fettuccine, cooked, drained and rinsed
12 shelled deveined cooked medium shrimp
1 cup green beans, blanched and cut diagonally into thirds
1 medium tomato, diced
4 scallions, diagonally sliced (reserve 1 tablespoon)

1 teaspoon whole-grain mustard
1 garlic clove, minced
1 tablespoon + 1 teaspoon olive oil
1½ teaspoons white wine vinegar
1 tablespoon chopped fresh tarragon, or 1 teaspoon dried
Salt and freshly ground black pepper to taste
16 lettuce leaves (Boston, Bibb)

1. Place fettuccine in large serving bowl. Cut each shrimp diagonally into thirds; add to serving bowl with green beans, tomato and scallions.

2. To prepare dressing, in small bowl, combine mustard and garlic. Whisk in oil until thick; whisk in vinegar until combined. Add tarragon, salt and pepper. Pour over fettuccine mixture and toss to combine.

3. Line four salad plates with lettuce leaves. Arrange fettuccine mixture evenly on each plate; garnish with reserved scallion.

EACH SERVING PROVIDES: 1 FAT; 1/2 PROTEIN; 1 1/2 VEGETABLES; 2 BREADS.
PER SERVING: 244 CALORIES; 14 G PROTEIN; 6 G FAT; 38 G CARBOHYDRATE; 89 MG SODIUM;
55 MG CHOLESTEROL; 6 G DIETARY FIBER.

REDUCED FAT AND SODIUM

163 Cellophane Noodle and Seafood Salad

Makes 4 servings

Versatile cellophane noodles studded with sesame seeds jazz up imitation crab meat with Oriental flavor. Use extra noodles in your next stir-fry.

1 package (87/8 ounces) cellophane noodles
12 ounces imitation crab meat, shredded
1 cup shredded zucchini
2 teaspoons toasted sesame seeds

1 tablespoon + 1 teaspoon sesame oil
1 tablespoon reduced-sodium soy sauce
1 teaspoon grated fresh ginger
1/4 cup chicken broth

1. Place noodles in large bowl; cover with boiling water. Let stand 5-10 minutes, until thoroughly transparent. Drain and rinse with cold water. Remove 2 cups noodles to large serving bowl (refrigerate remaining noodles for another use). Add crab, zucchini and sesame seeds.

2. To prepare dressing, in small bowl, combine oil, soy sauce, ginger and chicken broth. Pour dressing over noodle mixture; toss to coat well.

EACH SERVING PROVIDES: 1 FAT; 1 1/2 PROTEINS; 1/2 VEGETABLE; 1 BREAD; 15 OPTIONAL CALORIES.
PER SERVING: 343 CALORIES; 10 G PROTEIN; 7 G FAT; 63 G CARBOHYDRATE; 947 MG SODIUM;
13 MG CHOLESTEROL; 0 G DIETARY FIBER.

REDUCED FAT AND CHOLESTEROL

Tuna-Rigatoni Salad

Makes 4 servings

Need a fast dinner? This recipe uses ready-made dressing to cut preparation time.

4½ ounces rigatoni
2 cups broccoli florets
1 cup thinly sliced carrots
8 ounces drained canned tuna, flaked
1 medium red bell pepper, cut
  into strips
1 cup thinly sliced mushrooms

2 large plum tomatoes, diced
½ cup reduced-calorie Italian
  dressing (6 calories per tablespoon)
1 tablespoon Dijon mustard
¼ teaspoon freshly ground black
  pepper

1. In large pot of boiling water, cook rigatoni 10 minutes. Add broccoli and carrots; cook 4-5 minutes longer, until rigatoni and vegetables are tender. Drain and rinse with cold water; place in large serving bowl.

2. Add tuna, bell pepper, mushrooms and tomatoes; toss to combine. In small bowl, combine dressing, mustard and black pepper. Pour half the dressing over ingredients in bowl; toss to mix well. Cover and refrigerate 1 hour. Toss with remaining dressing; mix well. Refrigerate until ready to serve.

EACH SERVING PROVIDES: 1 PROTEIN; 3 VEGETABLES; 1¹/₂ BREADS; 12 OPTIONAL CALORIES.
PER SERVING: 257 CALORIES; 24 G PROTEIN; 1 G FAT; 37 G CARBOHYDRATE; 765 MG SODIUM;
24 MG CHOLESTEROL; 3 G DIETARY FIBER.

REDUCED FAT AND CHOLESTEROL

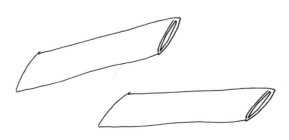

165 Herbed Salmon Salad Shells

Makes 2 servings

All the work you need to do for this easy recipe is to cook and fill the pasta shells. Pack them up for a take-along lunch or serve them on a bed of crunchy greens.

5 ounces cooked salmon, flaked
¼ cup finely chopped celery
¼ cup thawed frozen tiny peas
¾ ounce reduced-sodium Swiss
   cheese, diced
2 tablespoons reduced-calorie
   mayonnaise
1 tablespoon minced fresh parsley

1 tablespoon snipped fresh dill
1 tablespoon light sour cream
1 tablespoon fresh lemon juice
1 teaspoon grated onion
1½ ounces jumbo pasta shells,
   cooked, drained and rinsed
   (about 6)

In medium bowl, combine all ingredients except shells, mixing lightly with fork. Stuff shells evenly with salmon mixture, mounding slightly (about 2 tablespoons each). Cover and refrigerate at least 1 hour to blend flavors.

EACH SERVING (3 SHELLS) PROVIDES: 1¹/₂ FATS; 3 PROTEINS; ¹/₄ VEGETABLE; 1¹/₄ BREADS; 15 OPTIONAL CALORIES.

PER SERVING: 336 CALORIES; 27 G PROTEIN; 15 G FAT; 22 G CARBOHYDRATE; 176 MG SODIUM; 72 MG CHOLESTEROL; 2 G DIETARY FIBER.

REDUCED SODIUM

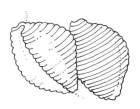

166 Sardine-Pasta Salad

Makes 4 servings

This salad can be prepared ahead and refrigerated overnight, which makes it perfect to bring to work for lunch. Full of good taste and very good for you, this salad provides 1,250 mg of calcium and almost 4,000 IU of vitamin A.

2 cups sliced red bell pepper
2 teaspoons grated lemon peel
1 tablespoon + 1 teaspoon
   lemon juice
1 tablespoon + 1 teaspoon olive oil

2 garlic cloves, minced
2 cups blanched broccoli florets
3 ounces elbow macaroni,
   cooked and drained
4 ounces drained sardines

1. To prepare dressing, in blender or food processor, combine half the pepper slices, the lemon peel and juice, olive oil and garlic; blend until smooth.

2. In large bowl, combine broccoli, pasta, remaining pepper slices and the dressing; toss to coat. Top evenly with sardines.

EACH SERVING PROVIDES: 1 FAT; 1 PROTEIN; 2 VEGETABLES; 1 BREAD.
PER SERVING: 216 CALORIES; 12 G PROTEIN; 8 G FAT; 24 G CARBOHYDRATE; 164 MG SODIUM;
40 MG CHOLESTEROL; 1 G DIETARY FIBER.

REDUCED FAT AND SODIUM

167 Chef's Salad

Makes 4 servings

A light dressing ties this salad together, chock-full of veggies, chicken, ham and two types of pasta. Experiment with different pasta shapes and flavors to find your favorite combination.

DRESSING:
1 tablespoon + 1 teaspoon olive oil
2 tablespoons balsamic vinegar
1 tablespoon chopped fresh parsley
1 tablespoon chopped fresh basil,
  or 1 teaspoon dried
1 teaspoon grated lemon rind
1 large garlic clove, minced
1 teaspoon minced chives
SALAD:
1½ ounces pasta shells, cooked,
  drained and rinsed
1½ ounces fusilli, cooked, drained
  and rinsed

2 ounces cooked ham, cut into strips
2 ounces cubed cooked chicken breast
½ cup sliced summer squash
½ cup sliced green bell pepper
½ cup blanched broccoli florets
½ cup blanched cut green beans
½ cup sliced fresh mushrooms
6 blanched asparagus spears,
  cut into 1" pieces
¼ cup sliced radishes
¼ cup sliced zucchini
3 cherry tomatoes, halved
¼ cup sliced red onion

1. To prepare dressing, in small bowl, combine all dressing ingredients.

2. In large serving bowl, combine all remaining ingredients. Add dressing; toss to coat. Serve immediately, or refrigerate to serve chilled.

EACH SERVING PROVIDES: 1 FAT; 1 PROTEIN; 2 VEGETABLES; 1 BREAD.
PER SERVING: 240 CALORIES; 11 G PROTEIN; 12 G FAT; 23 G CARBOHYDRATE; 186 MG SODIUM;
18 MG CHOLESTEROL; 2 G DIETARY FIBER.

REDUCED SODIUM AND CHOLESTEROL

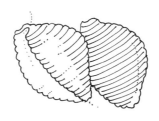

Turkey with Sesame Pasta

Makes 4 servings

Arugula leaves are a colorful backdrop for this dish, and their fresh, assertive taste is a match for the spicy sesame flavor. Cooked chicken works equally as well as the turkey.

2 tablespoons smooth peanut butter
1 tablespoon + 1 teaspoon red
   wine vinegar
2 teaspoons low-sodium soy sauce
2 teaspoons sesame oil
3 ounces spaghetti, cooked,
   drained and rinsed

2 cups cubed green bell pepper
1 cup sliced carrots
8 ounces cubed cooked turkey
Dried red pepper flakes to taste
2 cups arugula leaves

1. To prepare dressing, in small bowl, stir peanut butter, vinegar, soy sauce and sesame oil until smooth.

2. In large bowl, combine spaghetti, bell pepper, carrots, turkey and pepper flakes. Pour sesame dressing over pasta mixture; toss to combine.

3. To serve, place arugula leaves evenly on 4 plates; top evenly with pasta mixture.

EACH SERVING PROVIDES: 1 FAT; 2¹/₂ PROTEINS; 2¹/₂ VEGETABLES; 1 BREAD.
PER SERVING: 290 CALORIES; 23 G PROTEIN; 10 G FAT; 28 G CARBOHYDRATE; 163 MG SODIUM;
44 MG CHOLESTEROL; 4 G DIETARY FIBER.

REDUCED SODIUM AND CHOLESTEROL

169 Mexican Salsa Salad

Makes 4 servings

So easy, you'll want to make this dish again and again. Dress it up with a dollop of yogurt or light sour cream on each serving and a sprinkling of chopped cilantro or chives. Serve with nacho chips.

3 ounces elbow macaroni, cooked, drained and rinsed
1 cup chunky salsa
1 tablespoon red wine vinegar
1 teaspoon chili powder
½ teaspoon ground cumin

4 ounces drained cooked red kidney beans
3 ounces shredded Monterey Jack cheese
12 large pitted black olives, thinly sliced

In large serving bowl, combine macaroni, salsa, vinegar, chili powder and cumin. Stir in beans, cheese and olives. Cover and refrigerate at least 1 hour, until well chilled. Toss before serving.

EACH SERVING PROVIDES: 1/2 FAT; 11/2 PROTEINS; 1/2 VEGETABLE; 1 BREAD.
PER SERVING: 230 CALORIES; 11 G PROTEIN; 9 G FAT; 28 G CARBOHYDRATE; 606 MG SODIUM;
19 G CHOLESTEROL; 2 G DIETARY FIBER.

REDUCED CHOLESTEROL

170 Oriental Whole-Wheat Spaghetti Salad

Makes 4 servings

Crisp snow peas and broccoli with an Oriental dressing turn whole-wheat spaghetti into something special. A bonus time and work-saver is cooking the vegetables along with the pasta.

2 tablespoons tahini
  (sesame paste)
2 teaspoons rice wine vinegar
1 teaspoon honey
½ teaspoon ground ginger
⅛ teaspoon dried red pepper flakes

4½ ounces whole-wheat spaghetti
2 cups broccoli florets
1 cup snow peas
2 teaspoons sesame oil
2 large plum tomatoes, coarsely
  chopped

1. In small bowl, combine tahini, vinegar, honey, ginger and pepper flakes; set aside.

2. In large pot of boiling water, cook spaghetti 5 minutes. Add broccoli and snow peas; cook 4-5 minutes longer, until spaghetti and vegetables are tender. Drain and place in large serving bowl; toss with sesame oil. Add tahini mixture; toss to coat well. Top with chopped tomatoes. Serve warm or refrigerate to serve chilled.

EACH SERVING PROVIDES: 1 FAT; ½ PROTEIN; 2 VEGETABLES; 1½ BREADS; 5 OPTIONAL CALORIES.
PER SERVING: 223 CALORIES; 9 G PROTEIN; 7 G FAT; 35 G CARBOHYDRATE; 31 MG SODIUM;
0 MG CHOLESTEROL; 6 G DIETARY FIBER.

REDUCED FAT AND SODIUM; CHOLESTEROL-FREE

Bows with Herbed Crumbs

Makes 4 servings

Bow ties, those trendy little shapes, are curved to catch the garlic and herb flavored crumbs, a crunchy contrast to the tender pasta.

3 ounces small egg bows or
farfalle, cooked and drained
1 tablespoon + 1 teaspoon olive oil
2 slices white bread, torn into pieces
½ cup chopped fresh basil
¼ cup chopped fresh parsley

¼ cup chopped fresh cilantro
2 garlic cloves, minced
⅛ teaspoon dried red pepper flakes
1 tablespoon fresh lemon juice, or to
taste
¼ teaspoon salt

1. In serving bowl, toss pasta with 2 teaspoons of the oil. Let cool 15 minutes.

2. In food processor, process bread to form fine crumbs.

3. In large nonstick skillet, heat the remaining 2 teaspoons oil; add bread crumbs, basil, parsley, cilantro, garlic and pepper flakes. Cook, stirring constantly, 4-5 minutes, until crumbs are golden. Add crumb mixture, lemon juice and salt to serving bowl; mix well to coat pasta. Cover and refrigerate at least 1 hour, until well chilled. Add more lemon juice, if needed, before serving.

EACH SERVING PROVIDES: 1 FAT; 1¹/₂ BREADS.
PER SERVING: 164 CALORIES; 5 G PROTEIN; 6 G FAT; 24 G CARBOHYDRATE; 203 MG SODIUM; 21 MG CHOLESTEROL; 1 G DIETARY FIBER.

REDUCED CHOLESTEROL

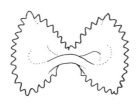

Desserts

Fruit, honey and nuts are some of the ingredients that can transform pasta from the usual main dish to a unique, decadent dessert. However, just because these recipes appear in this chapter doesn't mean they must be relegated to the end of a meal. Serving a sweet first course, such as Plum Good Pasta, with a main dish of meat or poultry, harkens back to the days when both sweet and savory dishes were served together. Jewish cooking has long paired sweet kugels with main meals as a side dish; try Noodle Kugel with poached fish and fresh asparagus to celebrate spring. Pineapple Noodle Pudding and Lemon Orzo Pudding are wonderful with a dollop of whipped topping or a sprig of fresh mint. Torta di Vermicelli is a torte-like pasta cake. Fruit salad lovers will enjoy Fruited Bow Tie "Ambrosia," full of juicy fruit, shredded coconut and miniature bow ties. Experiment on your own—create pasta desserts, using fruit or cocoa-flavored pastas (available in specialty food stores) and adding nuts, plump raisins and fruits cooked in wine or liqueur.

Apple Pie Bow Ties

Makes 4 servings

When you have a hankering for apple pie, this dessert can satisfy your yen nutritiously. Sift a teaspoon of powdered sugar over each serving, or top with a scoop of vanilla ice milk dusted with cinnamon.

2 tablespoons + 2 teaspoons reduced-calorie tub margarine
2 small Golden Delicious apples, halved, cored and thinly sliced
1/4 cup thawed frozen apple juice concentrate
1 tablespoon firmly packed light brown sugar

1/2 teaspoon cinnamon
1/4 teaspoon ground nutmeg
1/4-1/2 teaspoon lemon juice
3 ounces bow tie pasta, cooked and drained

1. In large nonstick skillet, melt margarine; add apples. Cook, stirring frequently, until apples are just tender, 2 minutes.

2. Add apple juice concentrate, sugar, cinnamon, nutmeg and lemon juice. Cook, stirring, until mixture is syrupy. Add bow ties; toss gently to combine. Serve immediately.

EACH SERVING PROVIDES: 1 FAT; 1 BREAD; 1 FRUIT; 15 OPTIONAL CALORIES.
PER SERVING: 187 CALORIES; 3 G PROTEIN; 5 G FAT; 35 G CARBOHYDRATE; 81 MG SODIUM;
0 MG CHOLESTEROL; 2 G DIETARY FIBER.

REDUCED FAT AND SODIUM; CHOLESTEROL-FREE

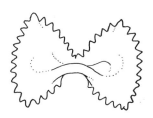

174 Fruited Bow-Tie "Ambrosia"

Makes 4 servings

Ambrosia, known as the food of the gods, is the inspiration for this fruit salad-pasta dessert with pineapple, coconut and honey.

3 ounces small bow tie pasta, cooked
  and drained
1 tablespoon honey
⅛ medium pineapple, cut into ½"
  pieces
3 medium fresh apricots, pitted and
  thinly sliced

¼ cup currants
2 tablespoons flaked coconut
2 tablespoons light sour cream
2 tablespoons whipped topping

1. In large bowl, combine pasta and honey. Add pineapple, apricots, currants and coconut; toss to mix well.

2. In small bowl, combine sour cream and whipped topping; stir into fruit mixture. Cover and refrigerate at least 2 hours before serving.

EACH SERVING PROVIDES: 1 BREAD; 1 FRUIT; 50 OPTIONAL CALORIES.
PER SERVING: 172 CALORIES; 4 G PROTEIN; 3 G FAT; 35 G CARBOHYDRATE; 11 MG SODIUM;
3 MG CHOLESTEROL; 2 G DIETARY FIBER.

REDUCED FAT, SODIUM AND CHOLESTEROL

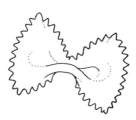

DESSERTS
Slim Ways with Pasta

175 Plum Good Pasta

Makes 2 servings

Sautéed plums with almond-flavored liqueur are combined with noodles and then topped with chopped nuts—a classic Italian flavor combination.

1 tablespoon reduced-calorie tub margarine
2 small firm ripe red plums, halved, pitted and sliced
1 tablespoon granulated sugar
2 teaspoons almond-flavored liqueur

1 teaspoon lemon juice
1½ ounces wide noodles, cooked and drained
1 tablespoon chopped pistachios or sliced natural almonds

1. In large nonstick skillet, melt margarine; add plums. Cook, stirring frequently, until soft, 3-5 minutes.

2. Add sugar, liqueur and lemon juice; cook, stirring frequently, until mixture is slightly syrupy. Add noodles; toss gently to combine. Sprinkle with nuts; serve immediately.

EACH SERVING PROVIDES: 1 FAT; 1 BREAD; ¹/₂ FRUIT; 55 OPTIONAL CALORIES.
PER SERVING: 197 CALORIES; 4 G PROTEIN; 6 G FAT; 31 G CARBOHYDRATE; 60 MG SODIUM;
20 MG CHOLESTEROL; 2 G DIETARY FIBER.

REDUCED FAT, SODIUM AND CHOLESTEROL

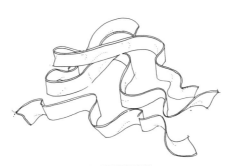

DESSERTS
Slim Ways with Pasta

Cheese Tortellini Suzette

Makes 4 servings

A dramatic dessert! Orange sauce coats the tortellini, which is then sprinkled with cognac and ignited. Give your guests a memorable treat and prepare this flaming dish tableside—carefully.

2 tablespoons + 2 teaspoons reduced-calorie tub margarine
1 tablespoon granulated sugar
¼ cup thawed frozen orange juice concentrate

1 teaspoon grated orange peel
2 cups cooked cheese tortellini
1 tablespoon cognac or brandy

1. In small bowl, combine margarine and sugar; stir in orange juice concentrate and orange peel.

2. In large nonstick skillet, heat orange juice mixture until bubbly and thickened, about 2 minutes. Add tortellini; toss gently to coat. Heat, stirring constantly, until sauce is syrupy and coats tortellini.

3. In small saucepan, heat cognac. Pour over tortellini; carefully ignite, using a long wooden match. Shake skillet until flames die down. Serve immediately.

EACH SERVING PROVIDES: 1 FAT; 1 PROTEIN; 1 BREAD; ½ FRUIT; 45 OPTIONAL CALORIES.
PER SERVING: 258 CALORIES; 10 G PROTEIN; 7 G FAT; 38 G CARBOHYDRATE; 335 MG SODIUM;
32 MG CHOLESTEROL; 0 G DIETARY FIBER.

REDUCED FAT

177 Noodle Kugel

Makes 4 servings

Save room for a serving of sweet kugel as a dessert, or try it as a wonderful side dish along side your holiday meal.

3/4 cup apple juice
1/2 cup egg substitute
1/4 cup + 1 tablespoon raisins
1 tablespoon honey
2 teaspoons vegetable oil
1/2 teaspoon vanilla extract

1/8 teaspoon allspice
1/8 teaspoon cinnamon
4 1/2 ounces wide noodles, cooked and drained
1/2 ounce sliced natural almonds

1. Preheat oven to 350°F.

2. In medium bowl, combine all ingredients except noodles and almonds. Add noodles to mixture; toss to coat.

3. Spray an 8" square baking pan with nonstick cooking spray. Spoon noodle mixture into pan; sprinkle evenly with almonds. Bake 30-40 minutes, until lightly browned.

EACH SERVING PROVIDES: 3/4 FAT; 1/2 PROTEIN; 1 1/2 BREADS; 1 FRUIT; 25 OPTIONAL CALORIES.
PER SERVING: 251 CALORIES; 8 G PROTEIN; 6 G FAT; 43 G CARBOHYDRATE; 50 MG SODIUM;
30 MG CHOLESTEROL; 2 G DIETARY FIBER.

REDUCED FAT AND SODIUM

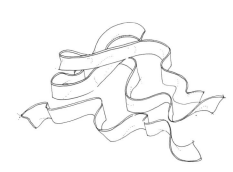

Pineapple-Noodle Pudding

178

Makes 4 servings

Make this easy three-step pudding when you find yourself hunting through your kitchen looking for something sweet.

½ cup apple juice
2 eggs, beaten
½ cup crushed pineapple
2 tablespoons granulated sugar
¼ cup golden raisins
2 teaspoons canola oil

½ teaspoon vanilla extract
Pinch cinnamon
Pinch ground nutmeg
6 ounces egg noodles, cooked
  and drained
2 teaspoons margarine

1. Preheat oven to 350°F. Spray an 8" square baking pan with nonstick cooking spray.

2. In large bowl, thoroughly combine all ingredients except margarine.

3. Scrape mixture into prepared pan; dot evenly with margarine.
Bake 35-40 minutes, until set and lightly browned.

EACH SERVING PROVIDES: 1 FAT; ½ PROTEIN; 2 BREADS; 1 FRUIT; 15 OPTIONAL CALORIES.
PER SERVING: 323 CALORIES; 10 G PROTEIN; 9 G FAT; 53 G CARBOHYDRATE; 65 MG SODIUM;
147 MG CHOLESTEROL; 2 G DIETARY FIBER.

REDUCED FAT AND SODIUM

179 **Lemon Orzo Pudding**

Makes 4 servings

If you like rice pudding, try this refreshing variation. Grate lemon lightly to get only the brightest part of the yellow peel.

3 ounces orzo, cooked and drained
2 cups low-fat (1%) milk
1 large egg
1 tablespoon + 1 teaspoon granulated sugar

¼ teaspoon vanilla extract
⅛ teaspoon salt
1 teaspoon grated lemon peel
Fresh mint sprigs and lemon peel to garnish

1. In large saucepan, bring orzo and 1½ cups of the milk to a boil, stirring occasionally. Reduce heat to medium-low; simmer, partially covered, 15 minutes, until orzo is very soft and milk is absorbed. Stir in the remaining ½ cup milk. Cook, stirring, until milk bubbles, 1 minute. Remove from heat.

2. In small bowl, whisk egg, sugar, vanilla, salt and grated lemon peel. Stir in a small amount of the hot orzo mixture, then stir back into saucepan. Return to heat; cook 2 minutes, stirring constantly, until mixture is thickened and creamy; remove from heat and let cool. Cover and refrigerate until well chilled. Garnish with mint and lemon peel.

EACH SERVING PROVIDES: ½ MILK; ¼ PROTEIN; 1 BREAD; 20 OPTIONAL CALORIES.
PER SERVING: 166 CALORIES; 8 G PROTEIN; 3 G FAT; 26 G CARBOHYDRATE; 147 MG SODIUM;
58 MG CHOLESTEROL; 1 G DIETARY FIBER.

REDUCED FAT AND SODIUM

180 **Ditalini Omelet**

Makes 1 serving

Not just for dessert—try this sweet omelet for breakfast or brunch with a piping hot mug of fresh French roast coffee.

¼ cup egg substitute
¼ cup ditalini (short tubular pasta), cooked and drained

⅓ cup 1% lowfat cottage cheese
2 tablespoons raisins
⅛ teaspoon cinnamon

1. In small bowl, combine egg substitute with 1 tablespoon water. Add ditalini and stir well.

2. In another small bowl, combine cottage cheese, raisins and cinnamon.

3. Spray small nonstick skillet with nonstick cooking spray; heat over medium heat. Pour egg mixture into skillet. Cook 3-4 minutes, or until set and edges are lightly browned; loosen edges with spatula. Remove from heat.

4. Place cottage cheese mixture over lower half of omelet. Slide omelet out of pan onto a plate, folding remaining half of omelet over filling.

THIS SERVING PROVIDES: 2 PROTEINS; ¹/₂ BREAD; 1 FRUIT.
PER SERVING: 181 CALORIES; 16 G PROTEIN; 2 G FAT; 26 G CARBOHYDRATE; 386 MG SODIUM; 3 MG CHOLESTEROL; 1 G DIETARY FIBER.

REDUCED FAT, SODIUM AND CHOLESTEROL

181 Torta di Vermicelli (Vermicelli Cake)

Makes 6 servings

This impressive dessert, prepared in a soufflé dish, will fill your home with the wonderful fragrance of orange and cloves.

¼ cup reduced-calorie tub margarine
4½ ounces dried vermicelli, broken into 1½" pieces
1 cup evaporated skimmed milk, scalded
¼ cup golden raisins
3 tablespoons + 1 teaspoon granulated sugar

2 tablespoons frozen orange juice concentrate
2 teaspoons grated lemon zest
½ teaspoon ground cloves
4 large eggs, separated

1. In medium nonstick skillet, melt margarine; add vermicelli. Cook over medium-high heat, stirring frequently, 5-7 minutes, until browned. Add 1 cup hot water and bring to a boil; boil 5 minutes, until pasta is tender.

2. Remove from heat; stir in milk, raisins, sugar, orange juice concentrate, lemon zest and cloves. Let cool slightly.

3. Preheat oven to 325°F. Spray a 1½-quart soufflé dish with nonstick cooking spray.

4. In small bowl, with electric mixer on high speed, beat egg yolks until thick and lemon-colored; stir in pasta mixture. In large bowl, with clean beaters, beat egg whites until soft peaks form; stir one-quarter of the beaten whites into pasta mixture, then gently fold in remaining whites. Do not overmix.

5. Pour pasta mixture into prepared soufflé dish; bake 55 minutes, or until puffed and golden brown. To unmold, invert hot cake onto platter; remove soufflé dish. Let cool to room temperature before serving.

EACH SERVING PROVIDES: ¼ MILK; 1 FAT; ½ PROTEIN; 1 BREAD; ½ FRUIT; 50 OPTIONAL CALORIES.
PER SERVING: 252 CALORIES; 10 G PROTEIN; 8 G FAT; 35 G CARBOHYDRATE; 184 MG SODIUM;
143 MG CHOLESTEROL; 1 G DIETARY FIBER.

REDUCED FAT AND SODIUM

Orzo-Cream Cheese Pie

Makes 8 servings

When you think you have a yen for a bakery cake, think again. This simple cheesecake-inspired pie is made with staples you'll find in your own kitchen.

3 ounces orzo, cooked, drained and chilled
1 cup raisins
¼ cup firmly packed dark brown sugar
2 ounces coarsely chopped walnuts

1 tablespoon all-purpose flour
1 teaspoon cinnamon
8 ounces reduced-calorie cream cheese
½ cup egg substitute
1 teaspoon vanilla extract

1. Preheat oven to 350°F. Spray a 9" pie pan with nonstick cooking spray.

2. In large bowl, combine orzo, raisins, sugar, walnuts, flour and cinnamon. In small bowl, combine cream cheese, egg substitute and vanilla; mix until smooth. Add cheese mixture to orzo; toss to mix well.

3. Spoon orzo mixture into prepared pan. Bake 30-40 minutes, until golden brown and set. Cool on rack 15 minutes. Serve warm, or refrigerate until chilled.

EACH SERVING PROVIDES: ½ FAT; 1 PROTEIN; ½ BREAD; 1 FRUIT; 35 OPTIONAL CALORIES.
PER SERVING: 213 CALORIES; 7 G PROTEIN; 7 G FAT; 33 G CARBOHYDRATE; 66 MG SODIUM;
4 MG CHOLESTEROL; 2 G DIETARY FIBER.

REDUCED FAT, SODIUM AND CHOLESTEROL

METRIC CONVERSIONS

If you are converting the recipes in this book to metric measurements, use the following chart as a guide.

VOLUME			WEIGHT		OVEN TEMPERATURES	
1/4 teaspoon	1	milliliter	1 ounce	30 grams	250°F	120°C
1/2 teaspoon	2	milliliters	1/4 pound	120 grams	275°F	140°C
1 teaspoon	5	milliliters	1/2 pound	240 grams	300°F	150°C
1 tablespoon	15	milliliters	3/4 pound	360 grams	325°F	160°C
2 tablespoons	30	milliliters	1 pound	480 grams	350°F	180°C
3 tablespoons	45	milliliters			375°F	190°C
1/4 cup	50	milliliters			400°F	200°C
1/3 cup	75	milliliters			425°F	220°C
1/2 cup	125	milliliters			450°F	230°C
2/3 cup	150	milliliters	LENGTH		475°F	250°C
3/4 cup	175	milliliters	1 inch	25 millimeters	500°F	260°C
1 cup	250	milliliters	1 inch	2.5 centimeters	525°F	270°C
1 quart	1	liter				

Dry and Liquid Measure Equivalents

TEASPOONS	TABLESPOONS	CUPS	FLUID OUNCES
3 teaspoons	1 tablespoon		1/2 fluid ounce
6 teaspoons	2 tablespoons	1/8 cup	1 fluid ounce
8 teaspoons	2 tablespoons plus 2 teaspoons	1/6 cup	
12 teaspoons	4 tablespoons	1/4 cup	2 fluid ounces
15 teaspoons	5 tablespoons	1/3 cup less 1 teaspoon	
16 teaspoons	5 tablespoons plus 1 teaspoon	1/3 cup	
18 teaspoons	6 tablespoons	1/3 cup plus 2 teaspoons	3 fluid ounces
24 teaspoons	8 tablespoons	1/2 cup	4 fluid ounces
30 teaspoons	10 tablespoons	1/2 cup plus 2 tablespoons	5 fluid ounces
32 teaspoons	10 tablespoons plus 2 teaspoons	2/3 cup	
36 teaspoons	12 tablespoons	3/4 cup	6 fluid ounces
42 teaspoons	14 tablespoons	1 cup less 2 tablespoons	7 fluid ounces
45 teaspoons	15 tablespoons	1 cup less 1 tablespoon	
48 teaspoons	16 tablespoons	1 cup	8 fluid ounces

Note: Measurement of less than 1/8 teaspoon is considered a dash or a pinch.

Index

Reduced Fat

Reduced Sodium

Baked Herbed Gnocchi with Tomato-Onion Sauce, 48

Baked Radiatore with Pesto Bechamel, 47

Baked Ziti with Red Pepper Bechamel, 46

Broccoli and Whole-Wheat Pasta Salad, 157

Cavatelli with Radicchio, Arugula and Bacon, 91

Chef's Salad, 167

Chicken-Avocado Fettuccine, 107

Chicken Tetrazzini Amandine, 56

Curried Chicken with Couscous, 144

Ditalini Omelet, 180

Fusilli with Walnut Cream Sauce, 81

Lamb with Orzo, 123

Lasagna with Fresh Tomato Sauce, 150

Lemon Orzo Pudding, 179

Linguine with Winter Greens, 87

Linguine-Vegetable Salad, 156

Macaroni Chick-Pea Soup, 35

Mexican Pasta with Beef, 131

Noodle Kugel, 177

Oriental Whole-Wheat Spaghetti Salad, 170

Pasta Primavera, 84

Pasta Shells with Lamb Sauce, 109

Pasta with Spring Vegetables, 136

Pasta with Tomatoes and Shrimp, 142

Pastitsio, 54

Penne with Grilled Vegetables, 90

Penne with Shrimp and Pepper Sauce, 99

Pesto-Stuffed Shells, 66

Pineapple-Noodle Pudding, 178

Pork and Rotini Casserole, 146

Pork Lo Mein, 112

Pork with Apples and Noodles, 145

Radiatore with Roasted Beets, Fennel and Onions, 86

Ricotta Pasta Salad, 160

Rigatoni with Sautéed Peppers and Basil, 89

Sardine-Pasta Salad, 166

Smoked Ham and Cellophane Noodles, 115

Spaghetti Pie, 57

Spicy Hunan Sesame Noodles, 114

Spicy Pasta with Broccoli, 141

Spinach and Shells Soup, 33

Torta di Vermicelli, 181

Turkey Ravioli, 67

Turkey Soup with Pasta, 38

Turkey with Sesame Pasta, 168

Whole-Wheat Fettuccine with Shrimp, 162

Ziti with Turkey Sauce, 104

Reduced Cholesterol